Gentle Lessons

FROM A RECOVERING PEOPLE PLEASER

Gentle Lessons

FROM A RECOVERING PEOPLE PLEASER

A Guide to Overcoming Obstacles to Peace

BY ALICE MCDOWELL

TATE PUBLISHING & *Enterprises*

The information herein represents the author's opinion only and is not intended to replace medical advice, psychotherapy or counseling. If you develop any difficulties such as, sadness, depression, or anxiety while doing the internal work and tasks required for the working of this process, it is highly recommended that you seek the professional help of a psychologist or doctor to assist you in your journey. The author and publisher are not responsible for any adverse effects or consequences resulting from the use or misuse of any of the suggestions or material in this book.

The opinions expressed by the author are not necessarily those of Tate Publishing, LLC.

Published by Tate Publishing & Enterprises, LLC
127 E. Trade Center Terrace | Mustang, Oklahoma 73064 USA
1.888.361.9473 | www.tatepublishing.com

Tate Publishing is committed to excellence in the publishing industry. The company reflects the philosophy established by the founders, based on Psalm 68:11,
"The Lord gave the word and great was the company of those who published it."

Cover design by Janae J. Glass
Interior design by Nathan Harmony

Published in the United States of America

ISBN: 978-1-60696-050-9
1. Self-Help: Personal Growth: Success
09.01.08

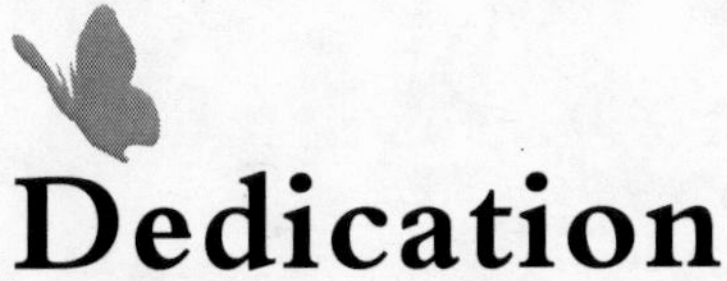

Dedication

This book is dedicated to my cousin, my little sister, my friend, Deanna DiOrio Goggins.

She strived for excellence her entire life, and was successful in her every endeavor, but her greatest gift was as a wife, a mother, and a friend.

She left us too early and we will all miss her.

Acknowledgements

I have much to be grateful for in my life and want to thank my wonderful friends, Lynn Jones and Carolyn Dillinger, for being in my life. Without their assistance and their encouragement, I would never have completed the manuscript. Their consistent presence, wisdom, and knowledge and enthusiasm throughout the process enabled me to persist in the writing and the finishing of this book. They generously shared their time, experience, and love, and I am forever indebted to them. And to my husband, Bob Trimmer, I bless him for his patience with my continual interruptions, and his computer literacy. His unconditional love has encouraged my transformation from chains to freedom, piercing years of repression. I am also grateful for the love of my daughters, Susan Monaghan and Jeanne La Marche and my wonderful grandchildren Connor, Lexi, Tiana, Dannie and Will. Their love and support is a gift and they are my inspiration. I also thank everyone at Tate Publishing for putting my book into print. Everyone was wonderful and fun to work with from start to finish.

Table of Contents

Butterfly in the Wind

A butterfly in the wind,
Some can fly higher than others
But each one flies the best they can.
Why compare one against the other?
Each one is different!
Each one is special!
Each one is beautiful!

Author unknown

Foreword

In 2007, when I was diagnosed with cancer, Ali McDowell rescued me spiritually and emotionally by offering me the same process she offers in this book *Gentle Lessons from A Recovering People Pleaser.* I was supremely impressed with her powerful process to help me discover and transform inner negativity. I didn't even know such negativity existed within me because it had never been uncovered by previous psychotherapeutic or personal-growth techniques.

The process Ali McDowell outlines in her book evolved out of forty years of study and work in nursing, social work, and spiritual counseling. Her process offers a transformational opportunity. Whether you are confronted with difficult times or simply a desire to expand your well-being, I promise that you will experience a dramatic shift toward greater happiness and personal freedom when you fully engage in the steps she outlines in this book.

Ali and I worked together as community mental health nurses in the early 1970s in Rochester, New York. Since then, though geographically apart, we always stayed connected, and last year after my diagnosis with cancer, she guided me in completing my personal chart, which is the foundation of the technique she uses. I was stunned to see the accumulation of negative thoughts and beliefs that emerged from within me, and with her continued support, I moved through a mind-expanding evolution. Personally, Ali is a warm, energetic, youthful-appearing woman whose smile lights up any room she enters. Her delightful passion for life is evident in her willingness to expend immeasurable time and energy in translating her inspirational process onto the pages that follow.

Lynn P. Jones, BSRN
Former Clinical Director,
Boardwalk Community, Denver, CO
Author of *A Matter of Community* and
A Matter of Community, Part 2
Las Vegas, NV

Introduction

"Our main motivation for living is our will to find meaning in life."

Viktor Frankl

Hi, my name is Ali, and I am a recovering people pleaser. People-pleasing and helping others was the essence of my life's work until I developed cancer at age fifty-seven. That was when I realized life as I was living it was not working for me; that realization was the beginning of the most challenging and rewarding journey of my life. My world was forever changed. What follows is what I learned, both from being a student and becoming a teacher.

If you have this book in your hands, it is not by chance. It means you are ready for positive change. The wisdom you gather and the transformation you will experience throughout this process is life long. The process offered in this book was developed by

Here I am, thirteen years after my second bout with cancer, holding my new granddaughter in 2006.

my personal life experiences in addition to forty years of practice in professional and spiritual coaching and counseling. This book provides a comprehensive step by step method to change your way of thinking, thereby shifting your thoughts, your actions, and your relationships. It also helps you identify your purpose in life. My book doesn't simply state what you must to do; it tells you how to accomplish sustained change. In that way, it differs from most other self-help books.

As Lynn Jones says in the foreword, whether you are confronted with difficult times or simply desire to expand your well-being, you will experience a dramatic shift in your happiness and life when you work this process. My sugges-tion to the reader, to increase and assure your success is that you first read the book in its entirety before you begin to work the process and the exercises. Being familiar with the total theory as well as the process helps you to better understand and achieve the principles of the process, making the exercises in the steps easier to accomplish.

It might also be beneficial to find a friend who is willing to work this process with you. Sharing your progress and helping each other with the questions in the exercises provides each of you another person who can comprehend and appreciate what you are attempting to learn. It would also be helpful in enhancing your self-awareness. Learning and sharing together with a friend is usually more fun anyhow. Lynn is a listening ear and always helpful to me as I am to her and it is wonderful to have someone that understands you.

Most of us don't know how to "do life better" or we would. When I say "do life better," I am advocating for living life with an easier, more loving approach towards yourself and others. "Doing life better" signifies possessing an awareness of how often during the day you feel hurt, angry, lose control, feel betrayed, judge or feel judged by others, judge yourself for doing something foolish or not looking good enough. "Doing life better" suggests that you know how to recognize all of the numerous and diverse elements that create and disturb your daily life. That recognition and awareness permits you to look at your life and your reactions to other people differently allowing you to change any behavior that is hurtful to you and others. When you are aware of what inside of you is creating your feelings and your actions you then have the power to choose another way, release negative choices and feel better about yourself. Your relationships in every avenue of life will vastly improve as will every element of your being.

During my first session with clients, I inevitably ask, "Why are you here on earth?" Fifty percent or more of the answers are, "I don't know. Good question!" The other fifty percent give me a general emotional answer resembling, "I am here to help others," or "I am here to take care of my children and my family." Not once has self-love or self-discovery or "I have a purpose" been an answer

Most of us tend to meander through our life experiences with little to no awareness of our greater purpose. We have no idea of the chaos we carry within and how that chaos creates the life we experience. At least I had no awareness of how often I had negative feelings and I was a successful nurse and counselor who counseled others. I also know this because of the thousands of interviews and intakes in my work of forty years as a psychiatric RN, spiritual counselor, life coach, teacher, and cancer survivor.

The majority of people, especially women I have met or counseled, have no appreciation of the importance of self-love and self-esteem in our society. There is rarely an understanding of the responsibility we possess to know, honor, and respect ourselves so that we can then offer the same love and respect to others and to the world at large. As a programmed people pleaser and one who had no concept of self-love, it rarely, if ever, occurred to me that I actually had a choice to please myself instead of making others happy.

The concepts and steps presented in this book formulate my personal process of self-love, developed over thirty-five years of counseling and teaching others. I had to identify my

Though I looked liberated and free in my thirties in this picture, I was first and foremost a people pleaser, an angry and hurt people pleaser.

own path to self love before I was able to foster others through the same process. I realized I could not teach what I did not know. If you observe others self talk and you are aware of how you talk to yourself you will find that you and most others are exceedingly self critical and unkind to yourself and others.

I was not a quick learner, had no idea of how to do life better and did not pay attention to my wake up calls (examples later in the book) so obviously I needed to experience a life threatening disease like cancer, before I discovered the meaning of my life. But you needn't learn through fear. You can discover positively through self-love. Only cancer made *me* feel a need to think differently, but you do not have to encounter disease to change your habits. After experiencing and surviving cancer twice, it was important for me to know why I was living on this earth in this body. The answers I found were simple though challenging. Living the answers requires and continues to command perseverance and determination because the solution is often contrary to society's teachings and its programming of children. Society generally and self-servingly teaches we must take care of others and that being selfish is negative and frowned upon.

I was an innocent three-year-old in this picture.

As early as three, I was told that I needed to make others like me so I was taught to smile and please my family first. To quote my mother, "God forbid that someone might not like you." Now I say that with a smile formulated in retrospect by love for my mother and affection for that little girl in the picture who needed love so badly.

Yet many years later, with loving guidance from a higher source, I was forced by cancer to find a path to self-love. For years, although I enjoyed life and had fun, I stumbled down a tough and trying trail. I kept looking for a better way to live, but it wasn't self-evident and I had no idea how to do anything differently. Cancer forced me to look in places previously unexplored—of all places, inside myself, my mind. I am sorry to say that never occurred to me! That is not what society or the Catholic Church taught me. I thought all my problems were outside of me, so that is where I looked for the answers. Scary too, is that's what I found in my many years of working as an RN, a counselor and a life coach. Everyone thought their problems were external and blamed others actions or words for creating difficulties for them. Friends, lovers, husbands, wives, bosses, jobs, children, school, traffic, and lack of money were all causing their problems. The list for blame seemed endless.

The inevitable happens when you look within. Its not scary, it is life enhancing and fun. When you dig deeper than the self-criticism, the judgment, your humanism, and the disappointment in yourself, you inevitably discover a goldmine. Your intuition, a higher power, and inner wisdom are just waiting to be discovered. At this point, the road becomes smoother. As many wise men and women teach, determination and perseverance, without doubt, will bring you success in any endeavor.

Self-love also means having the ability to forgive you for not being perfect. Self- love recognizes when you are critical and belittling of yourself, reverses the negativity and provides love and acceptance to you. Doesn't that sound wonderful? When you have acquired the skills to love yourself, you then have that same love to give to others. Life really is simple! If you are critical of yourself then you are more likely to be critical of others. You receive back what you give out. If you love and accept yourself, then you are more likely to love and accept others who, in turn, give you love and respect back.

Given that principle, I believe unconditionally that the basic and essential purpose of all human life is to foster and develop absolute self-love, self-acceptance, and self-respect. So life is not about becoming and remaining a people pleaser. It's not about being selfish or self-centered. It *is* about unconditional love for you first and then when you are proficient at self love, you grant unconditional love to others. You cannot give away what you do not own. If one doesn't possess self-love, one has no love to give to others consistently. Self love and love for all without exception, though difficult to achieve, is the only true path to peace and joy. It is virtually impossible to be unhappy, judgmental, or critical of yourself or anyone else when you possess self-love.

Dr. Bernard Siegel, a physician whose books and tapes helped me immeasurably through cancer, says it best in the foreword of *The Creation of Health* by Carolyn Myss and Dr. Norman Shealy. He asks, "What is our responsibility to ourselves and the cosmos? I believe it is all related to the role of love. Self-love and self-esteem are required. We must start with self-love and self-healing in order to be able to extend to others. Free will is the key ingredient to make it meaningful." Dr. Siegel was one of the first known western physicians to endorse the importance of self–love.

Because of my personal experience and my success in my work with others, I believe in the triumph of this process. However, through two bouts of cancer and various other life challenges such as marriages, divorces (notice the plural), child-raising, single mother problems, health issues, and death of loved ones, I uncovered the genuine reason I am in this body.

I've since shared my process with many, and through their hard work, they have transformed their lives as I changed mine.

Every narrative I write in this book is true. They either happened to me or to my clients. The stories may be hard to believe, but I neither could nor would invent such chronicles. Twenty years ago, before cancer, I was unaware of my personal power, a power that we all unknowingly possess. After experiencing continuing miracles over the last fifteen years, I am now an advocate. Believing in ongoing miracles is difficult for most of us, because we are unaware of the power of the mind and often we believe we don't deserve them.

Dr. Siegel also says, "The greatest reason to live the message is that it feels good. No one will live forever ... the longer one lives, the more loss one experiences. It is what you choose to do with the pain that is the choice." It is also what you learn from each experience that is important.

He ends his foreword with this vigorously endorsed advice:

"Open your eyes and mind to see, and you will believe. Do not let others tell you what you can see and believe. They will create defects in your visual fields that will lead you to deny what your collective unconscious has always known. Listen to that inner voice and be born again and healed in the true sense of the word. Let the creation of health begin in you."

I propose you follow the suggestions and process in this book and accept only my suggestions that resonate with your own truth. What follows is what I discovered thru my journey to my present beliefs and reality. While I was searching, I developed this process and I remembered what I had always known on a deeper level but did not believe possible. I can accomplish anything I choose to accomplish. My life has been forever changed. Strive for more, you can achieve it and you deserve it. You will have a new passion for life.

> *"The time for the healing of wounds has come."*
> Nelson Mandella, Inaugural speech 1994

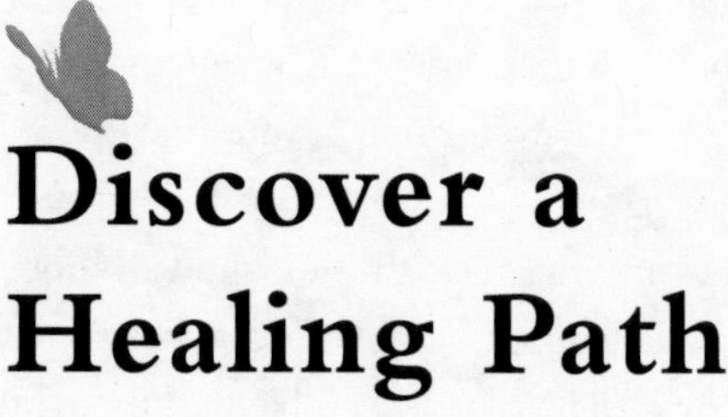

Discover a Healing Path

How to feel better

> *"Those who have a 'why' to live, can bear with almost any 'how.'"*
>
> Viktor Frankl

Viktor Frankl, a holocaust survivor, imprisoned for years in Auschwitz in the 1940s, refused to permit the Nazis to create fear in his mind and destroy him. Although they tortured his body, they were unable to affect his mind. He never feared them. Viktor Frankl said, "*The last of human freedoms is the ability to choose one's attitude in a given set of circumstances.*" He challenged the Nazi's, was persecuted by them, but survived the prison camp and maintained his self-respect. He suffered greatly at the hands of the Nazis, but he became a hero, an inspiration to other prisoners, and he never lost hope or control of his mind. He survived, was liberated, and lived long after the war to become a respected and successful author and speaker. Frankl is only one of the many examples that prove our mind is more powerful than any pain or torture. John McCain's prisoner of war experience is a contemporary example of mind over matter. Your mind is your most powerful asset so use it wisely.

In my earlier years—my twenties, thirties, and early forties—I never thought much about God. I was too busy having fun and working through life's typical problems. I thought life was about falling in love, possessing assets, and enjoying life's pleasures, and success. And I still believe that is a wonderful part of life but it never occurred to me that life was also about learning lessons and possessing self-love. I was successful, responsible, and a respected professional in my field. I worked hard, traveled the world, and generally enjoyed all that life offered. I was bright and intelligent but not a deep thinker. Not knowing any better, I chose the superficial path.

I looked confident but I wasn't.

As you can see by the picture, I had fun in spite of the fact that I was a second-generation Italian and that I was taught by parental example to be worried, guilty, scared, insecure, easily hurt, and in many ways timid, for fear of offending someone. Paradoxically, I also tended to be secure, optimistic, fearless, challenging, and felt I could accomplish any task presented to me.

So in 1994, at fifty-seven, when I was

diagnosed with breast cancer, a devastating shock and fear followed and then a gathering of my senses resulting in wisdom and a new awareness of the necessary changes I needed to make in my life. My first task in dealing with cancer was to identify the most respected and experienced doctors to treat me. I wanted doctors that I trusted implicitly who were experts in their field. Assisted by a family doctor that I had known for years, I quickly located knowledgeable doctors. Once that was accomplished, I felt driven to understand the emotional reasons that this was happening to me.

This picture with my dog, Parker, was taken during the cancer years.

Back in the '70s, while working as a nurse, people fascinated me because I recognized a connection between illness and anxiety. I studied and observed friends, coworkers, and patients in relation to what their circumstances were when they developed colds, flu, simple illnesses, or deadly diseases. Most of my friends were young and healthy in their twenties and thirties, but their bodies did react negatively to stress. As I watched, a trend emerged. Almost 100 percent of the time, their illnesses (and mine) were preceded by stress/anxiety, either physical, emotional, or a combination of both. My observations showed that people became ill after a traumatic experience with love, relationships, family, or work. To me, there was an obvious connection between problems, stress, anxiety, and illness. During the early 1970s in the medical profession, there was little to no connection between stress, anxiety, and illness. But, even so, I speculated that maybe those problems weakened the immune system, causing people to be more susceptible or vulnerable to colds, flu, etc. Since most were friends or acquaintances, I usually knew of any trauma that they were experiencing, so it was easy to observe if both elements were present.

With these collective observations in my consciousness, over time, I asked every client/patient and friend about stressful incidents in their lives prior to their illnesses. I noted that they frequently experienced an illness within six months of divorce or a death of a significant family member, arguments, or stress at work or home. Although I personally never did a formal study, I read several studies at the time that seemed to concur that stress could indeed negatively affect the immune system. A study of Harvard students, for example, tracked the levels and function of immune cells during periods of stress, and the results demonstrated that many different kinds of stressors, including preparing for an exam, relationship problems, and financial difficulties, led to a decrease in healthy immune cell function.

Another study by Ronald Glaser, PhD, Of Ohio State University College of Medicine and Institute for Behavioral Medicine and Research, compared 119 caregivers of spouses with dementia with 106 people of similar ages not living under this type of stress. Blood tests showed a chemical called Interleukin-6 sharply increased in the caregivers. Interleukin-6 has been shown to be associated with several serious diseases, including heart disease, arthritis, osteoporosis, type-2 diabetes, and certain cancers. The increase in Interleukin-6 was found to linger for as long as three years after the care-giving role had ceased. Dr. Glaser's article was published by Proceeding of the National Academy of Sciences.

Over the thirty-five years that I counseled people and observed the link between people's emotions and physical health, I became convinced that the mind affected the body. So when I developed cancer, I recognized I was no different than my friends; I knew I needed to explore how my thinking had affected my body. I was always a guilty worrier, and I finally realized fear and other negative emotions were stressing my body. Most importantly, I recognized the death of my mother from cancer had produced my worst fear, that I, too, would get cancer. For fourteen years I carried a fear of cancer and now it was my reality.

There had to be a link. I was determined to discover the connection and make the necessary changes within my mind, thoughts, and patterns of living. My discoveries were fascinating and empowering. In addition to Dr. Bernie Seigel, I found the work of MD's Carl Simonton, Andrew Weil, Vern Sylvest, and Deepak Chopra, all of whom I respected (see bibliography for titles). I listened to their tapes, read their books, and concluded that I carried a multitude of worries and fears. For the first time, I observed myself objectively and found I was not having fun, I worried too much, and I was way too serious.

In addition, I was always trying to be what others wanted me to be. Consequently I was filled with anger, worries, feelings of not being good enough, feelings of being alone and different. I also had a strong tendency to be critical and judgmental of myself and others. I was harsh with myself. Though I was a hard worker, I judged my appearance, my performance at work, and my abilities; I judged every aspect of myself. I realized I expected perfection, at which I frequently failed, and because I tried to be perfect, I expected others to be perfect. I judged others as I judged myself, but my harshness was mostly directed at me. In fact, my husband had been trying to tell me for years how self-critical I was and I couldn't hear it; my hair was too curly, my body was too fat, I needed to make more money. In my mind, I often did stupid things, and I was never good enough. The fact that I was enjoying an extremely successful career directing an agency for New York State did not seem to influence my opinion or decrease my negativity.

This was me at a party when I was receiving an award.

When I was able to recognize my negativity and lack of self-love, I discovered that I was horrible to myself. The enemy was me! I never would talk to anyone as I talked to myself. No wonder I had cancer! My overwhelming negative emotions were slowly eroding my self esteem, and left me with very little self-love. Others saw me as self-assured, bright, confident, successful, and even attractive, but that's not how I felt inside. And I always considered myself a positive person. I was, in fact, positive in that I believed I could accomplish anything, but I was also negative in my guilt, judgment, impatience, intolerance, need for perfection, worry; all very typical of everyone I have ever counseled or encountered. I learned the messages through programming from parents, school, and society. Underneath the facade, I was typically characteristic of society.

Notice me biting my lip in the picture?

I was only five, but I remember thinking that I was not "cute" enough when the photographer was taking this picture in grade school. Skilled at deceiving myself and everyone else with my positive, friendly exterior, underneath I was a worrier, negative, judgmental, and critical—all causing long-term damage to my mental and physical health. How do you talk to yourself? Consider that a serious question and think objectively to identify and recognize the many negative messages you may give yourself daily. Do you think you are too heavy or too thin? Do you complain about your hair? Any sports you don't play well enough? Are you not good enough at your job? Do you feel you should be better or more successful? Dou think you should perform perfectly?

> "What is this self inside us, this silent observer,
> Severe and speechless critic, who can terrorize us,
> And urge us on to futile activity.
> And in the end, judge us still more severely,
> For the errors into which his own reproaches drove us?"
>
> T.S. Eliot

Dr. Masaru Emoto, a Japanese physician, has researched water for over twenty years. His curiosity was that since the body is more than sixty percent water; he wanted a more comprehensive approach to understanding water. His research is fascinating as is his book, *The Hidden Messages in Water*. He sees water as a life force, a transporter of energy throughout our body. He says to understand water is to understand the cosmos, the marvels of nature and life itself. He has evidence that words, emotions, and both love and hate have a profound effect on water. His book is intriguing and shows you how your thoughts seem to be harmful to water and may be harmful to your body.

Dr. Emoto, in his experiments, put drops of water in hundreds of Petri dishes, and then labeled them with either loving messages (i.e., You are beautiful, I love you) or negative messages (i.e., You are ugly, I hate you). He and his staff repeated these messages to the water over a period of time and then froze the drops. When frozen, the water crystallized and the water given loving messages consistently formed beautiful white snowflake-like patterns, while the drops with negative messages consistently emerged as ugly, dark, unformed, or deformed. His conclusions were many, including one that established that water reacted to positive and negative statements differently. Since we are to a large extent composed of water, and because of his research, it is very possible that negative and positive emotions may be either helpful or harmful to our cellular structure.

I continued to read voraciously, especially books about the mind/body connection, that were written by leading western and eastern doctors who were also spiritual leaders. Dr. Bernie Siegel was especially helpful with his tape, *Preparation for Surgery, Radiation, and Chemotherapy.* I listened to his tape through surgery and treatments and have recommended it to many others facing cancer, surgery, radiation or chemo. It has always been helpful.

Change within came quickly. Once I started to practice affirmations and positive self-talk, it was easier to recognize and release harmful, destructive thoughts and practice what I was learning. A beautiful connection to God that had been buried by self-negativity was revealed, self-negativity that was generated by the years of unconscious conditioning and programming of society, parental and social expectations, rules, and structure.

The negativity within me was produced by societal training, social and marriage expectations, rules, parental hopes, sibling demands, teachers, friends, and structure imposed by every institution in the world in which I was involved. Structure, rules and training are not the culprits. The problem is that we as children are largely encouraged or expected to fit all of the molds created by those institutions. But we are not perfect and we all have different strengths so it is impossible to fit *all the molds* that are out there and there will inevitably be disappointment or failure to be perfect to confront us. Still we are raised to believe or we choose to have the expectation that we must fulfill these roles and/or accomplishments.

These beliefs and disappointments have been spawned in the minds of humans for thousands of years, predating Jesus' time. My intuition was always immediately available for others I counseled because I was listening without judgment, and now without judgment of myself, I could hear my intuitive and self guidance clearly. By now, I was able to recognize my negativity when it was present. I was beginning to respond more lovingly to myself and was able to forgive myself for being less than perfect. I was learning how to be gentle to me. Listening carefully to my instinct and insight changed my perceptions of me and others. I had always attempted to achieve my best but I now found that it was necessary to learn different, more constructive, and healthier coping mechanisms to be happy.

This was my personal experience in uncovering my intuition, and I felt that God was speaking to me; however, you don't need to believe in God to reach your power within. It is present whether or not you have faith in a God. This is an individual and personal decision, but this process works on everyone because it is about *you* and *your* power. We all have equal inner power; we just differ in the way we approach that power.

The process presented in this book includes my work, my discoveries, my lessons, and my success. It also worked successfully with clients. It does however take time, discipline, and effort to achieve the results I promise. Just as you will not have healthy teeth if you don't give them proper daily care, you will not attain peace and freedom without practicing all that this process requires. I continue to use a forgiving philosophy today and every day, though it is difficult to remember to forgive in a world that persists in presenting people or situations for us to judge. Merely observing the road rage present when driving for ten minutes offers multiple opportunities to judge other drivers or give one a reason to judge you. Believe the philosophy, practice the exercises, and use forgiveness with new insight daily, and it will work for you.

During my first episode with cancer, I walked every morning and listened to my intuitive guidance and heard messages to practice and follow. At the same time, while attending a spiritual group two to three times a week, I would hear the identical messages I heard earlier in the day on my walk, repeated in my group, either by the leader or another participant. After such concrete confirmation, I realized it was no accident that I was receiving the same messages from different sources. The group always reinforced the message without knowing I had heard it earlier. My trust in an inner guidance was growing and expanding.

I needed to help myself, and I was given the way daily if I listened. My learning was through experience and hindsight. I believe there are no accidents or coincidences. I trust that virtually every situation offers a lesson that I need to identify, listen to, and learn from. Every event and mistake presents opportunities and lessons for me. My challenge (and yours) is to identify the life lesson and the gift in every hardship or difficulty presented by life. In the early stages, this was neither easy nor always possible, but I *was* learning to see people, situations, and decisions differently. I had a choice; I could be positive or I could be negative. I could choose to see opportunity instead of mistakes. I could forgive myself and others or I could judge both. I could choose to like me or criticize me. Forgiveness and love brought joy and peace while judgment brought anxiety and disappointment, so I learned to forgive. I didn't always want to forgive. I am human, but I forgave because I knew it was healthier for me, my life and the people around me.

> "We cannot tell what may happen to us in this strange medley of life. But we can decide what happens in us—how we take it, what we do with it—and that is really what counts in the end."
>
> Joseph Fort Newton

My mother would be very proud! Now I am actually quite well behaved and well mannered with forgiveness.

After twenty-plus years of practicing my lessons, I am more consistent in my choices on a daily, moment-by-moment basis. The process is simple, but it is challenging. For me, it was the most stimulating and fulfilling, yet most demanding task I have ever attempted. Life offers so many reasons to judge and criticize, that I find myself continually challenged. Today I can still find myself judging or criticizing but I am more quickly aware that I am judging and therefore have the ability to forgive myself and choose differently. The spiritual trip continues to be rewarding. Until cancer, I wasn't paying attention to a higher purpose for living, but it is now the most important goal in my life. In early life I was lost in achieving, accumulating, and building a material life as I was trained. I had loads of fun, but I missed many opportunities to grow, so it took cancer to make me stop, listen, and learn. You don't have to develop cancer to learn to live differently.

With determination, I read enthusiastically and passionately. I utilized ideas and teachings from every book I read and every CD I heard. I accepted and practiced all that felt right or helpful and what made sense to me. Through this, I developed my own method for change over fifteen years. I was told that we teach what we need to learn, so as I learned and changed, I taught others. I had no one to coach me, so I created my own way. Everything I teach today, I needed to learn. That is truly a fact. In my ignorance I chose to learn the hard way, but you can make a different choice than I and create a new beginning today.

The process that I teach and practice is presented fully in this workbook. It is inspired by Roberto Assagioli, an Italian psychiatrist born in 1888, in Venice, Italy, whose theory was called Psychosynthesis. Assagioli was a contemporary of Freud and Jung, but in 1911 he moved beyond Freud, developing his own approach. He was the first to introduce the theory of the inner child and described them as sub-personalities. Dr. Assagioli believed there were multiple sub-personalities within each of us, creating havoc with our lives and behavior. Psychosynthesis is a spiritual, growth-oriented process that uses the whole-person approach. His concept and his intention were to bring a level of the unconscious to our conscious mind. This additional consciousness would allow people to make decisions from the higher self rather than reacting from lower emotions. Stephen Levine, a physician and author, states, "The investigation of healing is the path to joy."

My findings have been consistent with Dr. Assagioli's theory. Difficult as it is to believe, I and everyone that I have interviewed over the years hold within dozens of identical sub-personalities, though they may manifest differently in each of us. We feel so alone and separate yet we all have the same feelings, choose to play similar roles in life and have related beliefs. To name a few, we have inner rebels, people pleasers, super-achievers, super responsible, a failure, guilty, caregivers, hurt, not good enough, lonely, not respected, abandoned, disappointed, resentful, second-best, angry, etc.

I chose to call them inner children since most of our emotions and beliefs were formed at no more than one or two years of age. We develop personalities very early in life. And the inner children that rule our behavior and thoughts today need to be raised to maturity by giving them the unconditional love, acceptance, and security that they have never consistently received from family and society as children. As early as the first year of your life, your inner children were formed in your mind and started making decisions for you. You can take control of your spiritual, emotional and physical life with the insight and awareness gained in this process. It is difficult to make changes alone and we could all use some outside help. We need to learn to ask for help, either from friends, counselors, doctors or from God. When one asks for help, it is usually there for the taking.

> "*Asking for help doesn't mean that we are weak or incompetent. It usually indicates an advanced level of honesty and intelligence.*"
>
> Anne Wilson Schaef

With the input of forty-plus years of clients or patients and with cancer or other serious health problems, my evolution and a process of self-discovery developed and evolved. The process that follows works by uncovering specific self-sabotaging thoughts and actions and reveals your self-healing powers by identifying the layers of negativity within you that were generated by life and society. It then teaches you how to transform the negativity to unconditional love for yourself and ultimately others.

You view life through the emotional lens of a child until you remember and heal your early traumas. And, no, trauma is not too startling a word to describe the often destructive dynamics of how society programs children, even in the best of families. Your coping skills, both negative and positive, utilized by you today, emanate from childhood decisions and influences. Your perceptions and assumptions in childhood established the life-long responses and actions you continue to use today. We are all products of our environment, which includes teachings, approval by and disapproval of parents, grandparents, siblings, friends, teachers, and other experiences. Even as adults, we experience the events and people in our lives through the emotional lens of a child, emotions developed in childhood and adolescence. Dr. Carlos Warter, a psychiatrist, in his speech at the Omega Conference, Healing: *The Whole Self*, in Ft. Lauderdale, Florida, on November 7, 1999, said, "We need to heal the eye that sees through the filter of our emotional childhood, as we heal ourselves. We need to heal the misunderstandings with which we grew up."

Clients consistently say that they feel dramatically better after our first session because they can actually understand and see how they are creating their emotional pain. While you won't actually have a face-to-face session with me, my intention is to provide you with the tools needed to do this process on your own.

I believe, with good reason, that every cell in your body is affected by stress, anxiety, and sustained emotional pain that can or may produce physical pain. We each handle problems and stress differently. Identifying the sources creating your emotional pain empowers you to make different choices and create your life differently.

Many of my clients report that friends and family notice changes in their behavior during the first month of using this process. The success of the process depends on the amount of effort you dedicate to the questions and the work. Journaling is a major ingredient for success in this process. The more time you spend writing in your journal, the quicker you gain insight into your thoughts and habits. It takes diligence and determination to uncover the hidden parts of you, but the rewards are worth the effort. The many parts of you have been hiding successfully, creating chaos and confusion in your life for a very long time.

The Daily Guru writes,

> "*Who would allow you to totally ignore abuse, laugh with, swear at, shed tears on, get angry at and be totally honest with him/her? Your journal does. Your journal is an unconditional friend. It does not reject, manipulate, judge, laugh at or ridicule you. It is always there for you. So be honest with your best friend and it will help you discover who you are.*"

Below are several significant factors, roles and choices that can determine your decisions and help shape the outcome of your life.

Family expectations: Rules or assigned roles that are imposed at an early age on children or other family members that they are obliged to obey without question (the tribe/ family, teachers, bosses, friends, society and mass consciousness). These rules, teachings and expectations set the example for the family member no matter what age. Through this process, children often feel pressured to conform and are made to feel uncomfortable or inadequate when the roles are not followed and expectations are not met.

Conformist: One who conforms to family rules and assigned roles as best they can without honoring their individual preferences because of fear, rejection and or condemnation.

Rebel: One develops a stronger sense of self and ego by leaving or defying the expectations of others. They make decisions contrary to family rules and are judged and/ or ostracized by the family. The rebel will often leave the family fold or may choose to stay and continue to disrupt the family. The family will continue to try to change the rebel.

The Seeker: One who asks questions, challenges, and seeks independence from the family sometimes leading to rejection by the family. The tribe does not usually welcome change.

Awareness: One develops a spiritual insight and is able to hear their inner voice, guiding them.

Spirituality/Mysticism: One recognizes a higher consciousness, within the self as a part of God eventually resulting in self-love and service to others.

Where do you spend most of your time, and do you want

to shift to another level of being? In my teens, twenties, and thirties, I was clearly in society's mass consciousness. While receiving all A's in school and trying to live within family rules, the achiever role and the people pleaser role for fear of rejection, I was a slow, naive, learner. I had no awareness of the many emotions within me creating problems for me. I followed my family rules as presented to me, attempted to fulfill my parents' desires, and felt like a failure when I didn't meet expectations, both theirs and mine. I knew I could be hurt by critical comments and could fully feel sadness, anger, disappointment, irritation, and the whole array of feelings, but I had no idea that these emotions were destructive or that they could be changed. These feelings were "normal" for me. It never occurred to me that I could choose differently from my family, that I could make healthy choices for myself or that I could recognize situations that created negative and harmful feelings and choose my own unique way.

In one of my groups, while studying *A Course in Miracles*, the daily lesson was, *"I could see peace instead of this."* (Wb lesson 51) For the first time, I realized I *actually could* choose peace and see life and situations differently. When I read that statement, its significance pierced my consciousness and exposed a whole new world. I was amazed and surprised such a simple, straightforward statement with a clear concept could be so new to me at age fifty-seven. I began to look at every issue that challenged me from the perspective

of choice and I began to make conscious choices of what I was observing or experiencing. I frequently began to choose peace instead of anger or disappointment. It was healthier for me. I took my first step into awareness and quickly became a seeker. I loved and appreciated the freedom, the power and the challenge of being a seeker.

I began to apply this outlook to every situation or person that presented a challenge to me. In doing so, I chose what I wanted to see in any given circumstance, and I decided to see only the portion that felt good and release the rest as unimportant. My response was not denial; rather I had a myriad of choices to choose from in every situation that confronted me. This was a significant and fundamental step and became an essential component of my process. You always have a choice and your choices create your life.

> "You are free to believe what you choose and what you do attests to what you believe."
>
> A Course in Miracles

The damaging, destructive feelings, emotions, beliefs, and roles that I lived with for so long were finally wearing me down, and I was beginning to release them. I believe my body and immune system finally tired of carrying guilt, fear, anger, resentment, disappointment, hurt, stress, and dozens more negative feelings over many years kept eating away at me, eventually resulting in cancer.

In my work, I found that most people were as unaware as I, and carried the same emotions. As you work the process, you'll identify emotions and anxiety that stress your body and lower your immune system, building and feeding the foundation for disease. The process outlined in the book helps restore your emotional and spiritual energy by developing the necessary awareness of your emotions within. The steps reveal how your emotions and thoughts create your reactions and your life. Then you can decide who you want to be and in the evolution reclaim your internal wisdom. This is the beginning of real freedom and real power. Get yourself a beautiful journal and embrace the process that follows.

Please give yourself the time needed to answer the questions in each step of the process but try not to feel overwhelmed by the volume of questions and lists provided in the steps that follow. In my absence and to enable you to consider all the aspects I use when I personally help someone, I raise every possible issue and question for you to consider. You do not need to answer every question or identify with every item in the lists; simply select the issues that are significant to you. I also strongly suggest that you seek the assistance of a therapist to help you through this process, or if you are already seeing a therapist, share your work with him or her. It will enable you to move more quickly through the process and the feelings.

When a question or issue awakens an emotion in you, then it is significant, and you need to journal on it. If you feel no emotion behind the question, and if it doesn't seem to apply to you, leave it and go on to the next. The lists and questions are intended as inspiration for identifying emotions in your journal writing, and they represent the types of questions I ask clients when we meet in a counseling session. Consider each one significant and vital before you move on, because every question has the potential to unlock your subconscious as you move through the process. In your journal, answer all of the questions to continue to develop and increase your awareness. The more you write the more answers you receive and your self-awareness continues to expand with each answer. Since we really all feel the same inside, another enormous benefit with this process is that it helps you to see the humanness of others which in turn assists you in communicating with others.

Whether we appear to be rebels, bullies, or people pleasers, we all experience the same feelings internally creating our actions (i.e. hurt, anger, disappointment, scared, inadequate, etc). It is our choice of feelings that determine the difference in how we manage the behavior externally. To gain insight into your "feeling response" to others, feel your body's reaction when you get irritated or upset. Do you feel pain in your chest or in the pit of your stomach? Does your breathing get shallow? Do your shoulders or muscles tighten? Your body unfailingly reacts and tells you when you are not happy. Furthermore, if you want to understand and gain insight into the feelings of others watch and observe their actions or reactions. What do you see on their faces, in their body language, and hear in their words exposing their internal feelings? If you quietly observe others you will have a better understanding of what they feel. This observation and understanding changes how you choose to respond to others. It assists in developing your communication skills. These questions may raise your anxiety, so again, I strongly suggest that you find a therapist through your family doctor and seek help through your process.

Can you see any insecurity in the girls in the above picture? Outwardly they both appear pretty comfortable with themselves (and we thought we were). But the truth is both my friend Lynn Jones and I were people pleasers and unbeknownst to each other, always worried about the opinions of others.

This appears to be our rebel phase.

Step One

Developing awareness

Discover your buried treasures

Myth: We are aware of our thoughts and how our thoughts impact our lives.

Truth: Most of us have no idea of the enormity of negative feelings we carry within and how these feelings harm our health and our ability to "weather the storm."

> *"Just as the tumultuous chaos of a thunderstorm brings a nurturing rain that allows life to flourish, so too in human affairs times of advancement are preceded by times of disorder. Success comes to those who can weather the storm."*
>
> I Ching No. 3

⌘ Activity I: Begin writing! Step one is the foundation of developing awareness. Initiate the habit and process of writing about your feelings. Make it a daily or nightly habit. Natalie Goldberg, poet, teacher, and author of *Writing Down the Bones* says, "*The positive thing about writing is that you connect with yourself in the deepest way, and that's heaven. You get a chance to know who you are, to know what you think. You begin to have a relationship with your mind.*"

Step One: Look through your inner microscope and discover the buried feelings deep within. Embark on enhancing your awareness by recognizing and naming the many emotions within you. Any and all emotions are powerful because they influence your thoughts and perceptions and create your actions and your life today.

1. *Exercise:* Begin writing in a journal or notebook as soon as possible. Writing is renowned as a powerful and successful method of revealing the unexpressed and the unknown within you. *Do not underestimate the power of writing.* There is no limit. Write on anything. Write whatever comes to mind, especially negative thoughts or occurrences because this is your private journal. Ask questions of yourself and then write the answers.

What is she feeling?

Sample questions:

- How do I feel today?
- Did anything upset me today?
- What did I feel when I was upset?
- How did I handle it?
- Why did it bother me?
- What do I want to do about it?
- Was I happy today? If so what made me happy?
- Write your thoughts about yourself.
- Write your judgments of others.
- Write your opinions of life.
- Write what you hear in your head as you think.
- Write anything that helps you get to know your feelings and your beliefs.
- Write about your day, your thoughts, your life, your friends, or your activities.

Establish a routine of documenting your life. You control

your privacy so you can be free, open, honest, and candid. No one ever need see what you write.

Your journal plays an important role in completing the exercises, so do the assignments slowly and with thought. Sequentially, as you write, you build a deeper understanding and a clear analysis of what's inside, giving you a greater insight into what creates your actions, your reactions, and ultimately your life.

Focus on expressing your feelings in your journal, especially your destructive feelings (i.e., hurt, sadness, anger, guilt, second-best, alone, lonely). Research indicates that the expression of negative feelings has an immediate healing effect. You release negativity when expressing harmful feelings in your journal. It's healthier to express feelings in writing than holding them inside. According to many studies and in my own experience, writing about feelings is as effective as talking to friends. My personal belief is that it is healthier to journal than it is to talk to a friend about feelings. Friends and family, in their effort to help and support you, tend to feed and strengthen negativity. Journaling releases and is objective in that it is helpful, not harmful, and does not fuel negativity. Journaling is constructive because it allows you to express emotions safely and then transfer them from your head and body to paper.

2. *Exercise:* Make a firm commitment to write in your journal. Your happiness is worth at least fifteen minutes of your time every day, preferably at the end of the day. More time is better, but a minimum of fifteen minutes is a good beginning. Take as much time as you need. Here are suggestions to get started:

   Every evening before going to sleep, date and list all the feelings you were able to identify during that day.

   Describe any situation that took you out of peace and joy that created these feelings.

   Write about your day and document the variety of feelings you experienced.

   Examples are disappointment, anger, happiness, joy, irritation, judgment, hurt, sadness, resentment. If there are happy feelings, document those too and write about what created your happiness.

   Focus on your feelings rather than the circumstances or the other person and situation that created the feelings.

   Every evening, end the day journaling and finish your writing with three reasons for gratitude. Examples are, I am healthy, I am free, I have loving friends, I was able to help someone today, or I am happy to be alive. It could be as simple as "Someone smiled at me today." Always end your day on a positive note. Gratitude gives a healthful/helpful message to your body and cells, so initiate, promote, and create the experience of gratefulness as often as possible. Your body and mind will respond.

Notice each child's expression.

Study the faces in the picture to the left and observe each child individually. What do you see on each face? Each child in the picture is thinking differently about their activity. So it is with life.

3. *Exercise:* After one week, review your writings on the previous weeks' questions or topics. Identify and star (*) common or recurring feelings, behaviors, and areas of your life that have created problems for you in the past week.

   List them in your journal.

   While you are identifying these feelings, refer to the following Universal list of feelings, roles and beliefs and write all of the feelings in your journal that you believe apply to you.

   Distinguish between roles, emotions, and beliefs with the help of the Universal list.

   Name as many as possible (i.e., jealousy, irritation, insecurity, betrayal, sadness, hurt, disappointment, guilt, anger). The more you identify, the greater your awareness.

CHART ONE

Comprehensive List of Inner Children
Roles, Beliefs, and Feelings

Roles	**Beliefs**	**Emotions/ Feelings**
People pleaser	Aware	Angry
Victim	Second best	Unworthy
Need to be perfect	Not as talented	Invalidated

Roles	Beliefs	Emotions/ Feelings
Perfectionist	Not good at sports	Unacknowledged
Drinker	Not as interesting	Confused
Slut	Not as smart	Abandoned
Mother/ Father	Not respected	Invisible
Daughter/Son	Connected	Insecure
Oldest Daughter/Son	Playful	Judgmental
Protector	Secure	Critical
Fixer	Nice	Lost
Controller	Direct	Unlovable
Tag along	Faithful	Alone
Super responsible	Honest	Inhibited
Manipulator	Genuine	Scared

Roles	**Beliefs**	**Emotions/ Feelings**
Lover	Unwanted	Terrified
Responsible	Giving	Disassociated
Good Girl	Ugly	Unprotected
Super achiever	Fat	Inadequate
Artist	Independent	Hurt
Tomboy	Dependent	Sad
Bitch	Intelligent	Ignored
Betrayer	Not Cool	Different
Geek	Stupid	Jealous
Caretaker	Mean	Shamed
Clown	Unlikable	Lonely
Liar	Wrongly accused	Puzzled
Addict	Selfish	Clueless
Alcoholic	Concerned	Happy
Baby		Loyal

Roles	**Beliefs**	**Emotions/ Feelings**
Funny	Competent	Frustrated
Not good enough	Defensive	Resentful
Super achiever	Unlovable	Self-critical
	Judged	Rejected
	Impatient	

Important: If anger is one of the first emotions you identify, understand that there were many feelings accumulating prior to your feeling the anger. Anger is helpful as an emotion because it informs you of underlying, unknown feelings. There are dozens of emotions you experience quickly before you feel anger (i.e., fear/scared, not respected, second-best, ignored, not good enough, hurt, sad, betrayed, abandoned, attacked, irritated, defensive, etc.). These feelings pass though your mind so quickly, and so often, that you don't recognize the basic feelings because anger quickly becomes the dominant emotion. Anger itself is not a "bad" feeling. Inappropriate action as a result of anger is the destructive force that harms and wounds you and others.

Again, look at the faces in the above picture and notice the different expressions on each child's face. The girl and boy standing in the back look like they are not quite sure they are enjoying the activity. Each child has his/her own feelings as this picture was being taken. Notice the younger girl playing mother to the baby. Why is she doing that? Why does she want to? Why do you think she feels a need to take that responsibility? Then look at the older girl in the back row that does not look happy. What might she be thinking? Dig out some of your family pictures and look at yourself in all of them. Note your expressions. If your parents or grandparents are alive, ask questions of how they viewed you as a child. What were their thoughts about you? What made you passionate as a child? What made you angry? How did they see you interact with others? In that picture, as in life, everyone in the snapshot of life has a different perspective of each activity in which they engage.

4. *Exercise:* Be mindful of the times you say, "I would never" or "I should" or "he or they should." In using these words, you are judging others and yourself as well. Examine your professional and personal life and:

   List every action that made you angry or hurt in the last month.

   List any incident that takes you out of your peace and joy.

Be aware of how often you think or say "I should" or "I shouldn't." When you recognize them, replace the words with "I want" or "I prefer." And if you can't say I want or prefer, then you don't have to *do* your shoulds or shouldn'ts.

Choose to do only what you want; this is a major step to health for everyone but especially us people pleasers. This might sound radical and selfish, but if you want to shift your consciousness and live your purpose, beginning with this process, you must stop doing for others and do for yourself first.

If you continue to try to please others and don't do as you prefer, you simply continue to be angry.

Suspend disbelief at this point because sufficient reasons for this will follow later.

Remain open to all of your possibilities.

Allow compassion for yourself, get in touch with that passion, and write on the passion within you.

> "*The opposite of courage in our society is not cowardice, it is conformity.*"
>
> Dr. Rollo May, PhD, Theologian, Author

Note: This book is the beginning of a lifelong process and journey. It should be done at your own pace without guilt, taking the time you need to answer the questions thoughtfully, and your perseverance will reward you and lead you to the ability and peace to "do life" differently.

5. *Exercise*: Answer the key questions below that apply to you before you read on. Be patient and take as much time as necessary. Explore your mind and emotions as if searching for treasures. The more feelings you find, the more treasures and gifts you accumulate. These gifts assist in discovering more methods to help you. Write both the questions and answers in your journal. Francis Bacon says, "*A prudent question is one-half of wisdom.*"

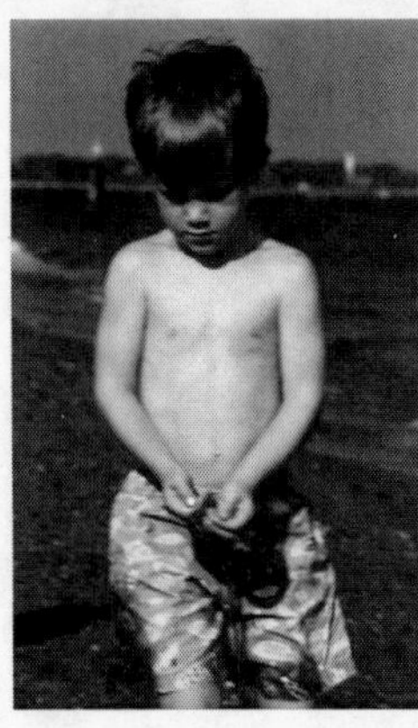

What is he thinking now?

- Are you experiencing relationship difficulties at work or home? If so, describe and write about the difficulties and how you feel about them.
- Are there teachings for you in this experience? Can you identify the teachings or lessons for you?
- What is the most important focus for you now?
- Is your focus on you or on another person's behavior? If your focus is not on you, bring the focus back to your feelings. Any time spent on another's behavior is a waste of your time. Focusing on how you could choose to respond differently is much more helpful to you.
- What would I feel if I knew I could not fail?
- What would I do if I had nothing to fear?

Do you ever feel:

- Alone
- Misunderstood

- A need to be perfect
- Guilty
- Not good enough
- Inadequate
- Something is missing in your life
- Sad
- Resentful
- Unappreciated
- Disappointed in yourself
- A disappointment to another

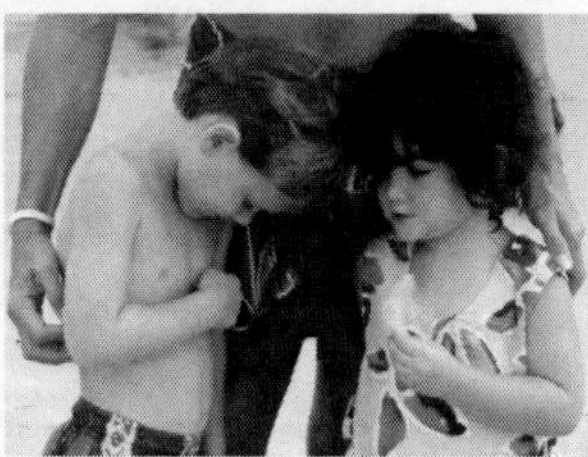

She looks very sad.

- Are you critical of yourself?
- Do you get angry if you make a mistake?
- What is the most loving action I could take or do now?

Write on each feeling and do not go on to the next word until you have exhausted the last feeling. Do the same with the following questions.

- When you feel sad, resentful, disappointed or any of the above, what do you do?
- How do you handle it? Is it helpful?
- What could you do differently?

When finished, read your answers. How do you feel about what you wrote? What did you discover about you? Identify and list your most common and frequent feelings. Review your writings and write on the insights you gained after reading your journal. Then document any changes you might choose to make in your thinking. Add any feelings, roles, or beliefs you identify to the list you started earlier. Your list should be getting longer as you go along the process. You may have over one hundred on your list before you are finished.

Feelings are interrelated and build on one another. Feelings change, come or pass quickly, and explain why we spend so much time feeling angry or sad. Peace and joy are your birthright. Do you feel peace and joy regularly? If not, you deserve to and you can if you choose your feelings wisely instead of unconsciously. Identify any feelings within you that may be destroying your peace and joy, and list them. When you understand the thoughts creating your actions, after noting them on your list, you can decide to change those negative thoughts and heal and release the thought patterns that no longer serve you. You gain peace and feel powerful! You can choose to see differently.

The goal of journal writing is to move your countless thoughts out of your head and on to paper. Journaling clears your mind. It also builds awareness and grants you the ability to discover and take control of the negative beliefs and thought patterns influencing your life and mind. We are *always* given the help we need but usually are unable to hear because our inner voices are speaking louder than our higher Self. The inner voices making all that chatter in your head are those same beliefs, feelings, emotions, and roles that you are identifying. Your findings are not to be judged, only accepted as an essential part of you. *Please don't use this as an opportunity to judge yourself.* You may wish to change some of those beliefs and roles, but none are terrible, just troublesome. The more beliefs and patterns you recognize and accept, the further along you are on your way to rebuilding your health and your life. You are as special as God created you so try to get in touch with the God part of you. It's inside you and worth the discovery.

After you have made your list and recognize as many emotion/feelings as possible, answer the following questions. When you are answering the questions below, look for the following three components within yourself: There will be some repetition of the following categories because they are important to remember and make it easier for you to identify all three.

Components of Self:

1. *feelings and emotions you have*, i.e., hurt, scared, angry, lonely, guilty, second-best
2. *roles you have played or roles that were given to you by others*, i.e., rebel, people pleaser, procrastinator, super achiever, caretaker
3. *beliefs you have of yourself and beliefs that others have of you*, i.e., you are selfish, you are lazy, you are smart, and you are always late.

As you answer the questions that are significant to you, list all of the emotions/feelings, roles, and beliefs that come to your awareness. This exercise should take several sessions because it involves time and thought. Time spent on you is not only crucial but invaluable because it supports your future health and happiness immeasurably. Devote as much time as necessary to your writing and answers. Be patient with yourself. Don't rush this as you have the rest of your life. Take several days if you need.

It can be life changing when you identify beliefs and judgments that are creating problems in your life. This part of the process is the foundation of your future happiness, so it is critical to identify as much as possible even though your list will grow as you move along. It is fun to discover you, so try not to deny or judge yourself as you uncover your thoughts. If you get stuck, ask people whom you trust to be gentle, to give you feedback on how they see you. Listen without judgment to feedback that you hear from others or see in yourself. Note everything only as important information that you need to identify to improve your future decisions. Again, write each question with the answer so when you reread in the future you will have a clear picture of your thinking and your feelings. As you develop your list of feelings, roles, and beliefs, they will be the foundation of your personal chart. Your personal chart displays all the internal turmoil, and is a tool you will be creating during the process and using throughout your life. Good luck, and I repeat, please do not judge any feelings you reveal to yourself! If you judge and dismiss feelings, you will omit a large part of you and compromise your learning.

6. *Exercise*: Important questions for you to answer while looking for roles, feelings, and beliefs: Take time for the following questions. It may take weeks for you to finish this list and that is fine. Don't rush through this process and the writing. There is no need to rush and wear yourself out.

7.
    - *When* do I criticize myself? (In what situations?)
    - *What* do I criticize in myself? For example: your looks, your weight, your relationships, your intellect, your accomplishments or lack of, etc. (list all and recognize when you are judging yourself)
    - *When* and *why* do I criticize others? (recognize as judgment and list why and when)
    - *What* do I criticize in others? (again, recognize these as judgments and see the common ones you use)
    - Do I compare myself to others and how does that make me feel? (competitiveness)
    - *How* do I feel when I am critical of myself? (list what feelings result from your personal criticism)
    - *How* do I feel when I am critical of others? (what feelings and what reasons for judging)
    - Do I ever feel inadequate or second best? If you had siblings as a child, did you count the gifts that each sibling received to make sure they did not get more gifts than you did? If so the fear of being second best started at a very early age. (Write about when you do and the reasons you don't feel good enough, list any role or beliefs by yourself or by others. Be aware of sibling rivalry and any feelings that might have developed in you as a result of siblings.)
    - What situations or statements make you doubt yourself? (Insecurity, names others might call you,

roles or beliefs, and feelings as a result of other's thoughts or beliefs about you. List all for your personal chart.)

- How did your parents or siblings or friends add to your self doubt?
- How did you feel about your parents when they disciplined you? (resentment, fear and anger, again, roles they put you in or that you assumed such as caretaker or fixer or clown, and beliefs sibling or parents had about you)

A typical family picture.

- Look at the faces of the family in this picture. Do they look happy? What emotions (or lack of) do you see that you can identify with?
- Did you choose to please your parents, or did you rebel? Which did you choose and why? List feelings.
- Were you allowed to show your anger? If not, did you

feel increased resentment and more anger?

- If you were not allowed to show anger, what did you do with it? Look at the frown on the baby on the right side of the page. Children usually smile. What might she be thinking?
- Did you feel alone or different as a child? If so why did you feel different and how were you different?

This is not a happy baby.

- Do you feel alone or different today? (Maybe feelings of being alone, not belonging, different, abandoned, scared? List all feelings that you can identify.)
- What do you believe will happen to you today if you break the mold your parents or society created for you or if you don't meet their expectations?

Read through your answers in your journal and add any new awareness (emotions, roles, or beliefs) to your list. Be generous with your time for yourself while completing this project. You may add any future thoughts or answers as they come to you. You have now completed the first step toward a new you. Good job! You are well on your way.

Step Two

Accept your feelings

It's okay to feel that way!

Myth: You must be positive and change all negative thoughts to positive.

Truth: You must be aware of and accept all aspects of your full self, including negativity, before you can make any long-term negative behavioral changes to positive. Denial of self does not work.

⌘ Activity II: *Okay then, feel that way*! This step is about accepting your feelings and then accepting yourself. Read all you have written in your journal to date and make lists of feelings you identify that you think are undesirable.

Step Two involves accepting and allowing all feelings as legitimate and important without judgment. Nothing about you is considered objectionable. It's essential to accept every part of you in this practice. When you judge and reject feelings that you dislike, then you are judging and cannot change your actions, thoughts, or behavior. This step is about accepting, even loving the many parts of you that have felt unloved to this point in your life. The hurting parts need to be given the proper love and attention from you that they never received consistently as a child. Once you have identified all of the hurting parts, later steps in the process will teach you how to love them and care for them. This step is only about identifying your numerous beliefs and feelings. It is essential to remember that when you look within, you accept and allow any guilt, shame, anger, disappointment, and other emotions recognized, without judgment. Judging your findings is detrimental to this process.

Set time aside to read your observations and writings.

- As you read your journal entries, how do you feel about you? Are you judging?
- Are there specific notes that generate heavy or negative feelings within you?
- Do you feel ashamed of any emotion you have identified? Why?
- Do your feelings create guilt?
- Are there issues that feel unfinished and in need of resolution?

If so, then you need to forgive yourself and accept every part of yourself with love and forgiveness. Self-forgiveness is easily accomplished by repeatedly saying, silently or out loud, "I forgive myself for not being perfect" every time you notice yourself being critical of self. You don't have to believe what you are saying; you just need to repeat that sentence over and over as you grow, learn, and change. You will begin to believe it and it is healthier for you.

It helps to say this same sentence about another person if you are thinking negatively about them. Say, "I forgive ______ for not being perfect. He/she is doing the best they can." Practice saying this sentence *every* time you doubt yourself or feel a need to judge yourself or judge another. At this step, you probably won't believe it all, but it's not necessary to accept all as true right now. It just needs to be said by you, to you in order to initiate the healthy process of forgiving yourself for not knowing a better way.

In my work, and in my own life, I found that our self talk is extremely critical and we would never speak to others as we talk to ourselves. We are brutally cruel and negative in our self talk and we would have no friends if we treated others as we treat ourselves. We have no respect for our own feelings. When I hear my teenage granddaughters, both of whom are outstandingly beautiful, tell me that they are fat, ugly, stupid, and not as good or as pretty as others, it makes me sad. They have no awareness of their external and internal beauty and spend their time feeling insecure and less that perfect. So have compassion for yourself, a child who was never taught how to cope with the problems life presented. You have been doing the very best you could in your life, and now you can learn a better method. The plus factor is that you no longer hold onto negativity. It is released through your writing and your self-forgiveness.

Study his face. What do you see?

Your goal, in this step, is to practice acceptance allowing you to accept feelings that you and others have criticized and judged in the past. All children learn early in life what are acceptable feelings and what are not. *In this process today*, we don't judge any feelings/emotions you discover and we accept all you identify. You may choose to change these feelings in the future, but at this point, practice acceptance. Many of us learned that expressions of anger, hatred, or resentment were unacceptable, while others may have learned that feelings of sadness, neediness, fear, or vulnerability were considered a weakness. Neither is true, love every part of you and embrace all of you. Now you can give yourself the unconditional love that you needed but did not receive as a child. By now, hopefully, you will have read Dr. Emoto's book on water and you recognize how harmful thoughts create disharmony in your cells.

You remain imprisoned by the opinions of others if you fear anger, rejection, objection, or disapproval. Your life and behavior will be controlled by family, friends, or strangers simply because they want you to be as they choose, not as you choose for yourself. Most people judge and attempt to control others rather than do their own work because they believe it is far easier to change others. It is not easy to develop self-awareness and change yourself. It is much easier to blame others or attempt to change others, and it often works for a short time at best, especially when it is people pleasers you are struggling to change. But you can never change another person unless they agree and most often they don't. It is quite effortless to generate guilt in people pleasers and they will try very hard to please others. Whether you are the people pleaser or you are trying to guilt a people pleaser, in the short run, it may appear that it is working. In the long run, however, it just creates problems, frustration, and failure for everyone involved.

You need a thorough awareness of your feelings and a total acceptance of yourself to live your purpose. After acceptance you can begin the process of choosing and allowing yourself to be whoever you want to be with joy and passion, regardless of what others may think. *This does not give you license to hurt anyone physically or emotionally. It is about honoring your own needs and taking any action that is legal that honors those needs.*

Fear of exposure of certain feelings and fear of rejection and/or disapproval were created because you undoubtedly encountered negative reactions by significant others in your childhood. Families tend to have spoken and unspoken rules about which emotions can be expressed and which cannot. Even if you didn't actually experience rejection or disapproval for these feelings, you probably made an early childhood decision not to express them, fearing rejection. It takes courage to accept all feelings, especially for those of us who want people to like us. This includes rebellious ones who frequently happen to be angry people pleasers choosing to act as rebels. Both are carrying considerable anger.

Accepting and changing negative feelings provides a wonderful sense of freedom. Awareness is essential because without knowing your feelings, it's impossible to reframe or change the negative to positive. If you're not aware of your thoughts and feelings, you can't change anything. First you need awareness and then acceptance—the first two steps of this process.

Denying your negative feelings is denial of self. Denial of self is different than knowing how you feel and consciously choosing not to express it. It is reasonable to choose how and when to express feelings you perceive negatively, but when you deny your feelings, even to yourself, you are denying who you are. Like most of us, you probably believe the naturally formed resentment that follows unexpressed or repressed feelings is caused by someone elses' behavior (projection), but in reality, you are choosing to deny your feelings and electing to blame others.

Projection is the most commonly used defense mechanism. The definition of projection that follows is by Richard Niolon, PhD, and from web page www.psychpage.com. Dr. Niolon writes,

> *"Projection is something we all do. It is the act of taking something of ourselves and placing it outside of us, onto others; sometimes we project positive and sometimes negative aspects of ourselves. Sometimes we project things we don't want to acknowledge about ourselves, and so we turn around and put it on others (i.e., "It's not that I made a stupid mistake, it's that you are critical of everything I do!") Sometimes it is simply our experiences (i.e., "My father was a reasonable man when we disagreed, so if I use reason with my boss we can work out our disagreement.")*

> *The problem of projecting negative aspects of ourselves is that we still suffer from them. In the above example, instead of feeling inadequate ((our true feeling) we suffer with feeling that everyone is critical of us. While we escape from feelings of inadequacy and vulnerability, we nonetheless still suffer and feel uneasy. The more energy you put into avoiding the realization that you have weaknesses, the more difficult it eventually is to face them."*

Projection is done unconsciously, without awareness. All defense mechanisms by definition are unconsciously executed. You project your feelings onto someone so you don't have to feel anything unpleasant because the blame is on them. However, the negative feelings remain connected to your problem and they remain in your mind. They are not released. The anxiety connected to the negative feelings remains inside of you, buried, and that same anxiety builds over time to create other difficulties in your life. Therefore, you are not creating your life consciously and you are completely unaware you are using a defense mechanism, thereby postponing or preventing your growth and stressing your body.

You hurt yourself by not owning your destructive feelings. It is normal in life to have negative, critical feelings. This process helps you recognize the presumed negative feelings, accept them, change them and honor all your feelings. You might want to explore defense mechanisms on the Internet. Dr. Niolon's page is excellent. Defense mechanisms are fascinating. Read especially about denial, projection, rationalization, suppression and repression but become familiar with all of them. Again, this would be a good time to seek help from a therapist and make this process easier for you.

Give your feelings a safe, private place to be released by transferring them to your journal rather than continuing to carry harmful feelings and thoughts, stressing your body. Accept your feelings, and note them in your journal. Relieve your body of a lifelong burden you have unknowingly forced it to bear. Be aware and be healthy.

The lack of awareness of negativity that lurks within is not unusual. Research has shown that suppression or repression of negative feelings affects your health and is the only psychological factor that appears consistently in disease and other research. For instance, a 1991 study from Melbourne, Australia, found that to a statistically significant degree, patients with cancer were more likely to demonstrate elements of denial and repression of emotions and avoided conflicts than those who did not have cancer. While I did not deny my emotions, I did suppress them as a people pleaser because I wanted others to approve of me. Over time, this suppression created significant anger within which I believe contributed to the development of cancer. Another study revealed that cancer patients have an unusually high tendency to control their emotions thereby creating disharmony within.

An interesting study in 1984 measured the physiological responses to stressful stimuli of three groups of patients: melanoma patients, heart patients, and patients with no medical illness. All of the patients were shown slides displaying unpleasant messages such as "you're ugly" or "you have only yourself to blame." The physiological responses, which were measured by a dermograph (a device that shows electrical reactions in the skin) were the same for all three groups, but the melanoma group was the most likely to deny any awareness that the messages had upset them emotionally. This study, from the book by Gabor Mate, MD, When the Body Says No; Understanding the Cost of Hidden Stress, reveals that the body registers upsetting reactions even when the mind denies being upset. Imagine the stress on the body when it is forced to cope for years and years with negativity that the mind refuses to recognize.

Candace Pert, PhD, researcher and author from Johns Hopkins University, believes that unexpressed emotions can cause illness. She says that unexpressed emotions literally become lodged in the body, stored in your cells in the form of peptides, or chains of amino acids. She further explains that it takes a certain amount of energy to keep the emotions from coming into consciousness. Inhibitory chemicals and impulses in the body serve to repress them. She stresses that intellectually becoming aware of feelings in the cortex or "thinking" part of the brain will not resolve anything. Your feelings need to be felt on a conscious level.

Love and accept yourself through this process. Stop pretending you don't care. Be yourself. It's time for change and change is rarely comfortable. It is time to make your life easier and more fun, lasting fun. But only you can do it. Life really is more enjoyable when you allow yourself to say yes or no without guilt. No matter where you are, bring your own sunshine.

> *"I find it fascinating that most people plan their vacations with better care than they plan their lives. Perhaps that is because escape is easier than change."*
>
> Jim Rohn

Step Three

Your inner children are born

There is baby boomer
within each of us

Myth: You are alone and separate in this world.

Truth: You have many separate inner beliefs, but you are one with your Creator and one with each other.

> *"Our Inner journey takes us through the following stages relative to love and fear:*
>
> *UNCONSCIOUS LOVE: When we are born, we exist as pure love but we are not conscious of our love.*
>
> *UNCONCIOUS FEAR: Our souls have set the stage for our evolution. As we grow, unconscious fears arise in our personalities that draw experiences to us that wound us.*
>
> *CONCIOUS FEAR: Our wounds bring pain and*

suffering that enable us to become conscious of our fears.

CONCIOUS LOVE: When we have suffered enough pain, we are motivated to move through our fears to consciously experience the love (God) that supports us all.

Love is but the discovery of us in others, and the delight in the recognition."

Alexander Smith

⌘ Activity III: Your task in this chapter is to suspend disbelief, trust in the process, open your mind and identify all the many little selves that live within you.

Step Three: In this step, you learn that the feelings and beliefs you identified in your journal are actually living inner selves. Whatever your age, you are part of the baby boom of inner children and many of these inner children rule your life. These scores of emotions, feelings and beliefs construct your daily life without your consciousness or approval. So your life is lived and created by multiple, unexplored, unconscious, toxic beliefs from early childhood.

Einstein said that you could not solve a problem on the same level as the mind that created it. At this point, it is important that you suspend old beliefs and abandon any limiting, preconceived ideas. Be open to accepting and welcome the thought that you have powerful, untapped abilities. Some of the greatest and most successful minds (including mine) believe that the mind is powerful and can accomplish any feat. Most of the greats of the past and present accept we can accomplish anything we choose if we use the power of the mind; Bill Gates and Donald Trump, Viktor Frankl, Winston Churchill, Franklin D. Roosevelt Jr., Abraham Lincoln, and Socrates among them. Suspend doubt, trust the concept that you possess the power I believe you have, and you *will enjoy* amazing rewards. You don't have to give up your beliefs, nor do I expect you will embrace all of mine. A powerful mind residing with or within this all too human body may be an unfamiliar concept, but it has worked for me and many others, and I believe it will work for you too. Give yourself permission and time to consider the ideas presented in this book. You can always return to old beliefs, but this process may change your life in ways you never dreamed possible. This system empowers you, so why not believe it?

Dr. Assaglioli, the Italian psychiatrist from the early twentieth century, introduced the possibility that the "whole" of who we are is the total of many different parts of our personality. This is different from a multiple personality, in that a person with multiple personality disorder is characterized by the presence of one or more distinct identities or personalities that take control of the individual's behavior, most importantly accompanied by an inability to recall their behavior or actions that is not ordinary forgetfulness.

My process for healing is based on the concept that within each of us are forty to one hundred inner selves, which I call "inner children." I have no investment in what you choose to call them. Name them whatever you choose; they could be viewed as inner children, inner selves, personality aspects, sub-personalities, inner characters, Guilty Guy, Critical Dolly, Angry Ted or any nickname that suits you. I recognize the inner child concept has been widely overused, but since all of these feelings, emotions, and roles were developed in your early years and remained as childlike feelings, inner children (ICs) seemed an appropriate title.

The creation of these inner selves began in childhood. By the time you were five, the foundation of your beliefs had already been instilled in you by society, parents, siblings, teachers, and friends, and by the time you were sixteen to twenty years of age, these beliefs were well-formed. It is during those formative years that your inner children were born. It would be a mistake or denial to assume because you perceive your childhood to be a happy time that you did not have self-limiting beliefs instilled in you. Children develop self-limiting beliefs, negativity, fear, and harmful habits even in the best-meaning families and communities.

This face shows many thoughts and feelings.

The following statements are a few examples to help you recognize how well-meaning families create insecurities in the tender minds of children. One of the many and most grievously overused phrase by parents, teachers, and significant others to children is, "I am disappointed in you." Well meaning maybe and intended to motivate, but a child feels a sense of defeat, failure, hurt, sadness, not good enough, and many more, for you the reader, to uncover.

This phrase alone has programmed many a child to feel a failure or not good enough about him/her, thereby adding to or reinforcing the development of multiple inner children.

Respect and validation of children is important but few children receive consistent respect and validation from their well-meaning but uninformed parents. Often children are teased about their insecurities. My father used to call me Porky because I always thought I was fat as child and teen (and twenties and thirties and up). Little did he know that he was programming me to continue that feeling throughout life. My self-perception was always that I was chubby, even though I was never really overweight as I now look back on pictures of me. Whenever I asked him to stop, he would laugh and say, "I am only teasing." In my mind, he never respected my requests or my feelings. I felt ridiculed as a teen. This continued until I was in my forties. By that time the damage was done. Teasing, while amusing to the teaser and the observer, is generally detrimental to a child's malleable and tender self-image. Today I hear children teased constantly by parents, siblings, and friends. It is destructive to children who have sensitive feelings and who tend to believe what they hear factually. Those are only two of the many examples of parental habits that present negative programming to children. More examples will be identified later.

This picture speaks volumes of what children are thinking.

Devote time and thought to possible negative programming that you received and are able to identify in your life. Mothers and fathers, siblings, or friends don't recognize how detrimental teasing is to the child/adult being ridiculed. What made you feel second best or not good enough? What hurt your feelings or made you sad or angry? Look at the above picture and notice the expression on the older and the younger child. What do you see?

So who's making your decisions—who is choosing how to react? Is it the five-year-old in you or the eighteen-year-old in you? For your health, it's time to release old patterns, get to know yourself better and consciously decide to choose positively and become proactive rather than reactive. Why should you accept that there is just one of you?

Your inner children are outside your awareness, yet they make decisions for you and speak for you in defensiveness, anger, guilt, or insecurities and more. Imagine the resultant chaos in a room filled with forty to one hundred children with no controls applied. That's what your mind carries and creates today and every day.

Each of your inner children has a different belief about:

- who s/he should be (i.e., good or rebel, good enough/not good enough, smart, successful, lazy, outstanding)
- who s/he is i.e., smart or stupid, cool/not cool, worthy/not worthy
- what s/he isn't i.e., interesting/not interesting, pretty/not pretty, thin, not thin
- what s/he should do in any given situation i.e. please others or not, rebel or conform
- what s/he deserves i.e. punishment or praise, worthy or unworthy
- what's right i.e. selfish or sharing, shoulds or shouldn'ts
- what's wrong with you or others (your perceptions only)
- feeling respected or not respected
- how s/he should look (pretty or handsome or not)
- how others should look (perfect or not, any judgment of others)
- the consequences if s/he breaks the mold
- how and when to approach parents

So many different faces, so many different thoughts.

Once you know who's speaking within you and for you, you increase your understanding of how you alone create your daily pain/ anger/ happiness/ sadness). Make no mistake; you create your life and your anger as you go blithely through life, unaware that you are creating chaos within, usually resulting in problems in your relationships. You are much more powerful than you feel and you need only align all of your inner selves with the higher part of you to claim your power. That is not an easy accomplishment and a never-ending process, but it can be done with perseverance and is well worth the effort. You can be proactive and choose differently than you have in the past. Without the chaos inside, it's easier to recognize and achieve your life's desires and purpose. The good news is that you can change your life anytime you choose, once you have the tools.

> *"I do not know what I may appear to the world; but to myself I seem to have been only like a boy playing on the seashore, and diverting myself in the now and then finding a smoother pebble or a prettier shell than ordinary, whilst the great ocean of truth lay all undiscovered by me."*
>
> Isaac Newton

Exercise: This exercise helps you to recognize your inner children. Review your writings, and as you review, create a separate list of all the *feelings and emotions* you can identify, both negative and positive. Examples are: happy, scared, abandoned, not good enough, alone, betrayed, irritated. Add to the same list all of the *beliefs and thoughts* you have about yourself (fat, stupid, ugly, alone) and all of the *beliefs* others have about you (i.e., selfish, stubborn, sweet, smart, stupid, pest etc.). And finally, add any *roles that you have placed yourself in* (i.e., caregiver, rebel, super responsible) and *roles that others have given you* (i.e., proper son, smart daughter, hero, failure, good boy, good girl, achiever, underachiever). For assistance with this exercise, see Chart One on page 53: A Comprehensive List of Universal Children. List the roles, beliefs, and feelings that apply.

> *"If you want things to be different, perhaps the answer is to become different yourself."*
>
> Norman Vincent Peale

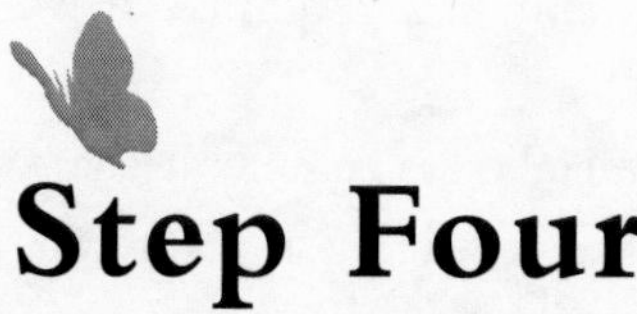

Step Four

Connect with your inner rascals

Free the kids

Myth: You are in control of your life.

Truth: The majority of the time, your inner children, programmed and created during your childhood, rule your decisions and actions, and in so doing, create and control your life.

⌘ Activity IV: This step is the beginning of the development of your own chart. Examine the Universal Children Chart and begin to identify and name your inner selves.

Step Four: This step identifies your inner children in preparation for Step Five, the creation of your own personal chart of your inner children (referred to as ICs in future chapters). Building your personal chart will be the foundation for your awareness and the completion of the process. Since there are so many distinct and common voices within us, I have developed and included what I believe to be a Universal Chart of inner children to help you identify feelings that are familiar or similar to your feelings. The next page will illustrate that the feelings you discover are common and normal. It will also help you create your own chart.

The Universal Chart shown embodies commonly shared feelings, regardless of race, color, age, education, status, religion, or sex. It speaks for one hundred percent of charts developed in workshops and private sessions with clients over the last fifteen years. The Universal Chart of inner children evolved with the help of people as young as seven and as old as seventy-five. They all admit and relate to having similar feelings and emotions summarized in the Universal Chart. Without much thought you could say, "Those are not my kids. That's not me." But consider the possibility of the existence of these feelings and emotions within you and list in your journal all the feelings, beliefs, or roles that relate to you, in preparation for developing your chart. The Universal Chart and the comprehensive list of inner children are tools to help you recognize and identify the feelings you have had in your life. In the center circle of the Universal Chart, you will see "inner wisdom" or "higher self" surrounded by all the inner children. When your inner children are active in you, it's difficult to hear your intuition, higher self, or inner wisdom. The thoughts/voices coming from the inner children surrounding your inner wisdom block your ability to hear your higher self. Your inner wisdom/higher self whispers assurances, while the children shout, criticize, take away your self-confidence, and tell you what you *should* and *shouldn't* do.

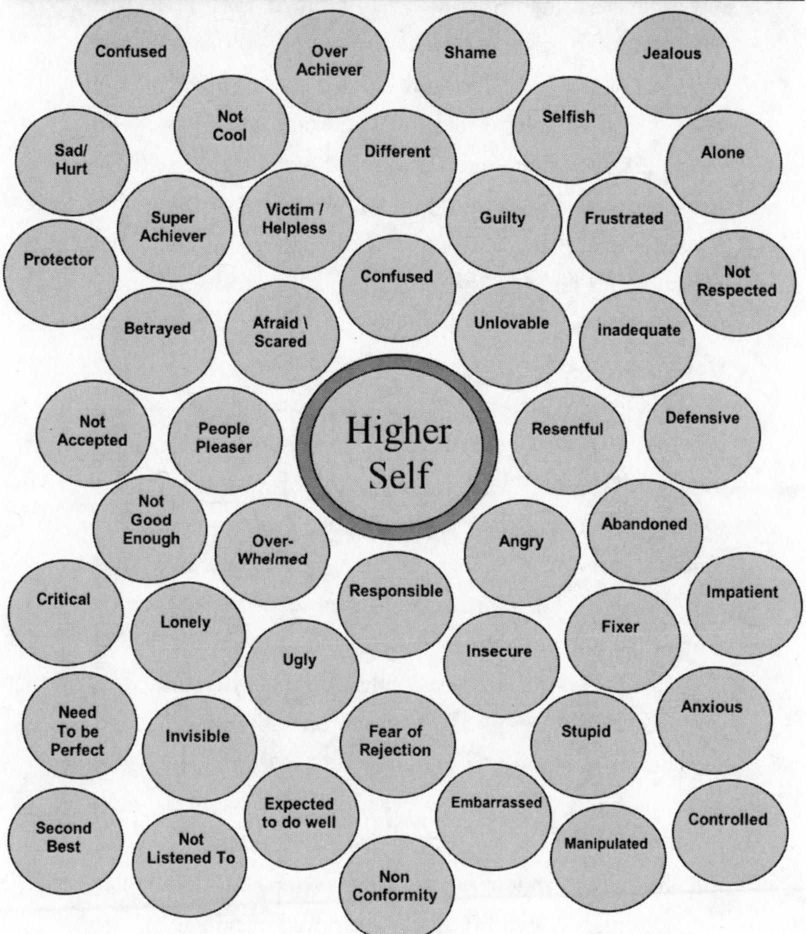
Universal Inner Children
Confused
Over Achiever
Shame
Jealous
Not Cool
Selfish
Sad/ Hurt
Different
Alone
Super Achiever
Victim / Helpless
Guilty
Frustrated
Protector
Confused
Not Respected
Betrayed
Afraid \ Scared
Unlovable
inadequate
Not Accepted
People Pleaser
Higher Self
Resentful
Defensive
Not Good Enough
Over-Whelmed
Angry
Abandoned
Critical
Responsible
Impatient
Lonely
Fixer
Ugly
Insecure
Need To be Perfect
Invisible
Fear of Rejection
Stupid
Anxious
Expected to do well
Embarrassed
Controlled
Second Best
Not Listened To
Manipulated
Non Conformity

When you are aware of all of the negative thoughts that are so universally present, you may feel that "life is hard." Life doesn't have to be difficult. It can be joyful and filled with abundance. You have a choice and can actually choose how you experience every day and build it as you like. But first you must to be able to recognize and take control of all the voices inside you in competition with your higher self. You really are your higher self, but the programmed inner children dominate the whisper of your higher self. In human behavior and feelings, the answers to all questions are internal not external. We look for love in all the wrong places when it is always within, just a thought away.

This handwritten partial chart is an example of how your personal chart takes form as you begin the process of identifying your IC's. As you fill in the circles in your chart continue to write all around the page if you need more room. Think kindly and try to *see through the eyes of a four, five, six, or seven-year-old child* while you complete these exercises. It's important to remember you were only a child when these feelings originated. When I am personally working with someone, I find they usually deny, make excuses for, and protest, defending parents by stating, "But I know they loved me, they didn't mean anything." The client becomes defensive, feels guilty, thinking they are being disloyal. I need to remind them continually that as an adult, they do know their parents loved them, but as a child they didn't always feel loved or remember they were loved when they were lost in the moment of anger, fear or hurt. Children and even adults, while they may know they are loved on one level, still have doubts and fears witnessed by the insecurities most of us still feel today. That was one of the

Example of chart by you. Name

Appendix B
Universal Inner Children

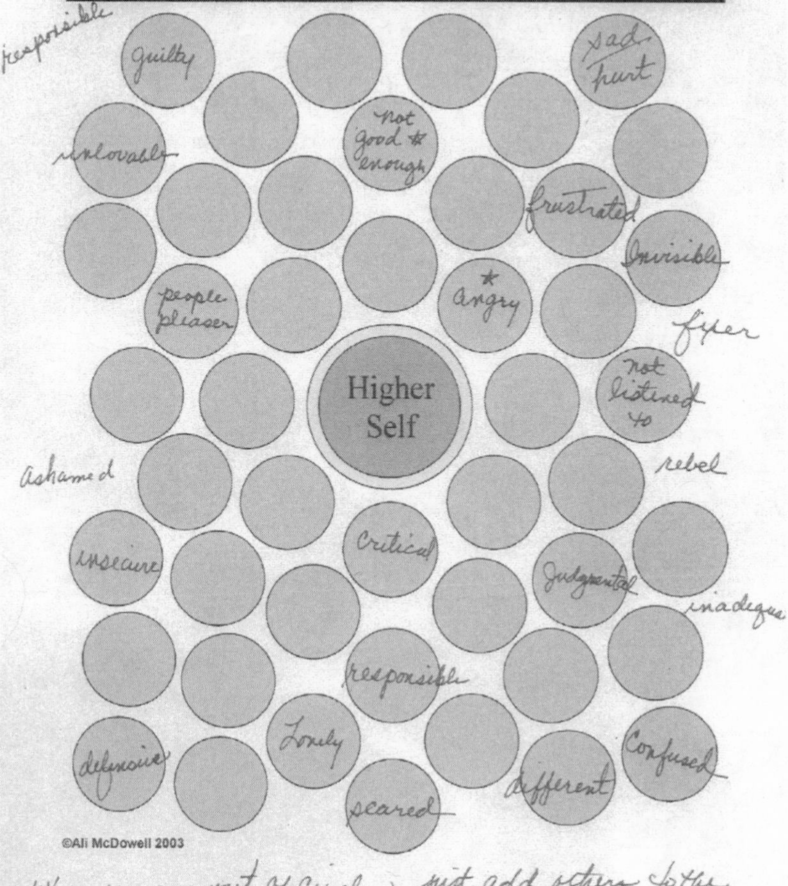

Higher Self

When you run out of circles, just add others to the sides as I have many reasons my clients were seeking counseling; their behavior was creating problems for them and they wanted to feel better about themselves and their lives. Curb your defensiveness. This is not about blaming parents, siblings, or anyone. As parents, we all do the best we can with the knowledge we have about raising children. This is about being honest and objective so you can better recognize and manage old feelings and emotions. How exactly are our "inner children" formed? They are derived from three main areas:

A. roles *you play or have played or roles you have been put into by others*
B. beliefs *you have about yourself and that others have about you*
C. feelings and emotions *in reaction to events today from childhood*

7. *Exercise*: List in your journal any feelings, beliefs, and roles you identify from the lists below as you read through the following examples. You may continue to use the earlier charts for inspiration as well as the examples listed below.

Examples:

Roles *you played or were given by others.* The following are all roles you might have chosen.

- Good Girl/Bad Boy or vice versa
- Rebel
- Selfish (not a bad thing)
- Fixer
- Caretaker
- People Pleaser
- Over/Under achiever

This picture speaks volumes.

The comments that follow are roles others gave to you such as:

- You're an angel.
- That child is a devil.
- You're selfish.
- What a brat.
- You are stupid.
- You are ugly.

Is this child an angel or any of the others?

List statements that you have heard said to you or about you in your lifetime. Add them to your journal and list any feelings as a result of hearing them.

Beliefs ***you have or that others have about you***

Parents might have told you that you were:

- intelligent or slow
- not as good a boy/girl as your brother/sister
- a disappointment
- unable to accomplish something
- not good enough
- selfish

Siblings regularly insult and call each other:

- stupid
- ugly
- pest
- fat
- not cool
- geek

Peace for a time.

Negative messages from others, repeatedly given to you in childhood, have a lasting impact on your self-esteem. Beliefs are also born from critical statements you make to yourself such as:

- I was really stupid.
- I feel second best.
- I blew it.
- My sister was Dad or Mom's favorite.
- I feel invisible.
- No one pays attention to me.
- I'm not important.
- Nobody cares about me.
- I'm not good enough. (*This one is common in everyone I have ever talked to.*)

The critic in you sits on your shoulder, constantly judging, always ready to remind you of every task you have ever performed that wasn't good enough, and asks, "Who do you think you are?" "You can't do that, you aren't good enough." "That is way too hard for you." Often the conditioning of not feeling good enough originates from you, not someone out side you. This programming has been present in your life since you were able to reason, make a determination or draw a conclusion. The many voices inside of you are constantly in conflict and all become part of your beliefs about yourself and how worthy or unworthy you are.

Your emotions and feelings

A. Emotions and feelings resulting from your response to events that happened "to you": (*emotions and beliefs* are in italics)

- I *feel sad* because Mommy is mad at me. (*feeling scared, not liked, not loved, bad*)
- I'm *confused* (feeling) because my brother is mean to me.
- Why doesn't my brother like me? (feeling *not good enough or unloved*)
- I'm *scared* (feeling) they don't love me or they will leave me. (*unloved, afraid, and abandoned)*
- She *doesn't love me* (*unloved*) because my grades *aren't good enough.* (both feelings)
- I'm *not good enough.* (feeling) because *I disappoint* my parents. (belief)
- *Nobody listens.* (belief)
- *Nobody cares what I feel.* (belief)

- I'm *not respected* because they are always telling me what to do. (feeling or belief)
- I'm *invisible.* (feeling)
- I'm all *alone.* (feeling and belief)

B. Emotions and feelings are also derived from trauma including any kind of:

- Sexual, physical, or emotional abuse
- Emotional or physical abandonment, family addictions
- Family illness, both physical and mental
- Any other dysfunction
- Divorce
- Death
- Betrayal by friends or family
- Severe anger or mental illness in either parent
- Parental mental illness or disability of a family member

All are traumatic and may cause long-term emotional damage to children. Children tend to respond to any event (i.e., divorce, damaging behavior by parents or siblings) personally and blame themselves. Children will frequently and irrationally blame themselves for divorce or a death of a family member. In blaming themselves, they focus on what they (the child) have done to create the problem. Add any emotions, feelings, roles, or beliefs to your list in your journal as you identify them.

C. Emotions and feelings resulting from snide, destructive, or malicious statements such as: (feelings in italics)

- You're adopted. (very commonly told to the youngest child by older siblings creating *a different and insecure* feeling within the youngest)
- I hate you. (also very common and creates a feeling of being *unloved or unlovable*)
- You should know better. (creates *stupid or not good enough* feelings)
- Stop crying or I'll give you something to cry about. (my father's personal favorite) (*not respected or not validated*)
- Nobody likes you. (*unloved and unlovable*)
- Get lost. (*not wanted*)
- Pest. (role)
- Go away. (*not wanted, insecurity, not liked*)
- You are stupid. (*stupid, not smart, not respected*)
- I don't care what you think. (*not important and not respected*) another of my fathers favorites
- You're not important. (*obvious*)
- I'm disappointed in you. (*a disappointment or a failure and ashamed*)

These are powerful statements, programmed by significant people over time creating the belief that you're not lovable and not good enough. When you do get an occasional validation, you don't believe it. Typically, if we receive ten compliments and one criticism, we tend to negate the ten positive and focus on the one negative. When I would hold workshops and received the completed opinion questionnaire, if 98 percent were positive and 2 percent were negative. Guess where my focus was? Why do we do that? Because we don't believe we *are good enough*.

I could have been the poster child for what I teach.

8. *Exercise*: Roles, beliefs, feelings, and emotions also have their source in the society in which you were raised as well as the society in which you live as an adult: Identify any negative messages you feel from the following examples and list in journal.

Society's destructive roles and rules for children:

- Children should be seen and not heard.
- You must share your things.
- Don't be selfish.
- You must always be nice no matter how you feel.
- Don't cry or I will give you something to cry about.
- Be a big girl/boy.
- Do as I say, don't do as I do.
- Why can't you be like as your sister/brother?
- One day you'll be sorry.
- Your face is going to freeze like that.
- You should know better.
- Go to your room; I can't stand the sight of you.
- Don't do that because ________ won't like you.
- I'm going to call the policeman and he will take you away!
- You can't help how you are.

Recognize any of these from your childhood? If any are familiar, note them in your journal and add them to your personal chart.

These messages create a feeling of non-respect and stifle a child's feelings.

Society's stigmas and roles for adults: Again, list any feelings identified in your journal.

- You need to have a partner or something is wrong with you.
- To be a man means you must be responsible for the happiness and welfare of your wife and children.
- Men don't cry.
- It's not normal to live alone.
- You must fit into society's idea of a responsible adult. (Whatever that might be)
- It's the woman's responsibility to have dinner on the table for the family.

These roles might seem out of date but are still alive and well in today's world and place additional unnecessary pressure on an already stressed child or adult.

A need to conform to convention and obedience are similar to society's stigma and can create the following inner children: List any with which you identify.

- people pleasers
- overachievers
- underachievers
- confused
- inadequate
- defensive
- guilty
- not good enough
- overly responsible
- anxious

- feeling alone
- feeling different

Critical or lenient parents: Society and parental choices vary from the extreme of excessive control or discipline with children to over-leniency. Critical and controlling parents can destroy a child's self-esteem and create anger, while overly lenient parents can make a child feel unloved and unimportant. A child feels out of control without structure. If you have children of your own that you are raising, know that structure gives children a feeling of comfort and safety and helps prepare them for responsibility in life. *Structure and discipline are necessary, need to be given with consistency and provided with love and respect for the child. Consequences for negative actions or broken rules should also be part of the equation.* Most children are very receptive and learn with security when all seven elements are included: love, respect, validation, structure, discipline, consistency and appropriate consequences.

Consider your own family and the era in which you grew up, and write any insights that you gain in your journal. Include respect and validation when disciplining your child by using recognition and respect for their feelings such as "I understand how you feel and I care about how you feel but when you break a rule there are consequences." Use statements like "I love and respect how you feel but these are the rules."

Make notes in your journal and take from these lists that which has meaning for you. The notes you write will help you fill in your own chart, in Step Five. Your personal chart is the foundation for changing your feelings and reshaping your life. You'll begin to recognize the same feelings and emotions in others as you identify them in you. Relationships will change, and your communication skills will improve. You can employ all that you learn to improve your relationships with your own children, as well as your inner children.

Once you are satisfied that you have an in-depth list with as many roles, beliefs or perceptions, and feelings that have meaning for you, move to the next step, and begin the process of creating your own personal chart of inner children.

Step Five

Creating your personal chart

Wow, can that be me?

⌘ Activity V*: Create your personal chart of the beliefs, thoughts, and feelings that live within you. This chart is the tool that will set up the process to be more apparent and real to you.*

Step Five: This step will *wow* you and is most important because you develop your personal chart of inner selves to expand your awareness, identify how your ICs choose for you and how they affect your life. Once you see the multitudes on paper and recognize that they represent all the activities in your mind, you will wonder how you were able to cope with daily activities. Utilize the list and all of the above charts to assist you when creating your personal chart. If possible, enlarge Chart C (empty circle chart) by copying it and enlarging it to at least 8 by 11 inches. If you can't enlarge the chart, use a blank 8 by 11 inch paper and draw your own circles so you have enough space. When you are inserting the feelings, roles, and beliefs into the circles, put them in any circle. There is no special place for any of them. Just insert the words as they are identified and star any that are particularly active in you. The only significance of the circles is to hold the feelings and show how they surround and drown out your inner self.

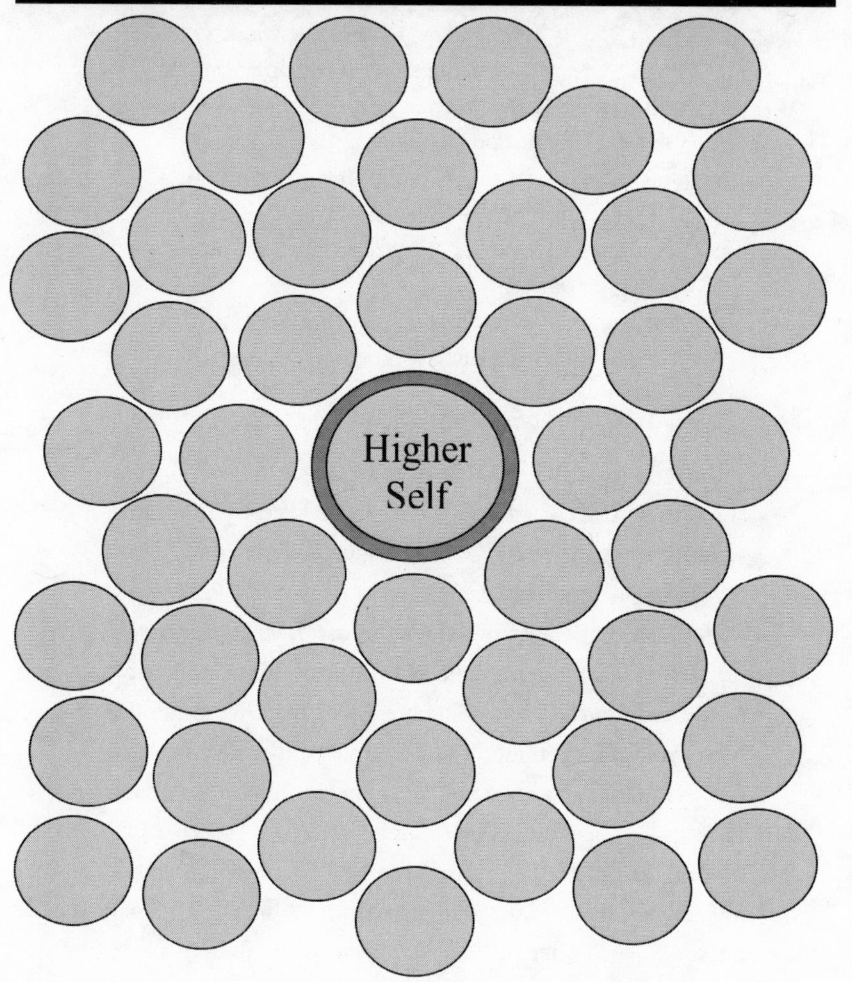
Universal Inner Children
Higher
Self

9. *Exercise*: Before you begin there are three more questions to answer. Document your responses in your journal.

    - Do you believe in any of the following: God, or a Creator, or a higher wisdom or power, or intuition? If the answer is no, do you at least believe in intuition?
    - Do you believe that God or Creator or intuition is within you or that you are a part of them or it? Do you feel there is a connection between you and a higher power?
    - What is your reason for your life here on this earth? What is your purpose and what are you here to accomplish?

Please give these questions time and thought. In teaching sessions, more often than not, the response I received for question number three was, "Good question, I don't know." Most clients know if they believe in God or a higher power, but few (if any) can state their life's larger purpose. If you are uncertain of your reason for being here, it is difficult, if not impossible to live a content and rewarding life. Many of us live unfulfilled lives without a meaningful sense of purpose or destiny. How can you fulfill a destiny if you don't know you have a purpose? How can one be fulfilled without an objective? It seems a set up for guaranteed failure and the result is disappointment. Write your answers in your journal after thinking on each question. I will offer you *my* answers to these questions later. Some say, "Ignorance is bliss." I believe wisdom and purpose add happiness to one's life. Most lives are not blissful.

In the center circle of your personal chart, write your own

words for your higher power, soul, God, inner wisdom, intuition, or higher intelligence. You may use any term that feels right to you that denotes a power higher than yours.

Next, fill in the other circles in the chart with every feeling/emotion/belief/role you have identified thus far from the lists in your journal. You may add to your chart at any time during this entire process. Use the Universal Chart and the more complete list of possible roles, beliefs and emotions/feelings to identify any and all feelings you have experienced. Add them to the list you created in the last exercise. After you have examined the Universal Chart and the possible list, record on your personal chart all you have recognized as being significant to you. You will continue to add to your personal chart throughout this book from past and present experiences.

Include any feelings, beliefs, and roles that you are aware of from the past. Include those you feel you have worked on, regardless of how much self-help work you have done to date. If the feeling ever existed in you as a child or as an adult, it is still a part of you and needs to be included. For example, if you think you have removed your guilt, include it in your chart anyway. If you ever had feelings of guilt in you, the feeling remains within. Perhaps not to the degree they did, but the feelings are still part of you. Remember specific roles, beliefs, or emotions that might have created past experiences, i.e., feeling that you should tell someone that they are wrong in their beliefs or you feel that you are disappointing your spouse or parents. After each example, as you fill in the circles in your chart, briefly describe in your journal how you felt in childhood or feel in present day.

Self-honesty and non-judgment are essential to the success of this process. Please don't judge any feelings as positive or negative. As the Tao says, they just are. The Tao is neutral. Your feelings may have been painful, but they are not negative, and I recommend that you accept them as a part of you. Include your perception of positive qualities too, i.e., happy, nice, caring, giving, smart, responsible, successful, and secure. When you consider whether or not you are judgmental and critical, ask if you have judged yourself ever. If so, fill in the circles with both. Also include if you have been judged.

Commonly you will have reverse characteristics/feelings in your chart. For instance, you might have both smart/stupid, secure/insecure, impatient/patient, tolerant/intolerant, loved/unloved/unlovable, happy/unhappy, bright/dull. Having opposites in your chart is normal because we live in a world of dualism. The more opposites you find, the more complete your chart will be. You may be tolerant of some traits and intolerant of others. Therefore you are both. There are times you may be impatient with some and at other times very patient depending on whom you are dealing with. If so, you are both. Retrieve a picture of you with a group of children. If you can find a photo with a few children in it, observe the faces and clothing of the children and notice how different each looks. Imagine how each might feel.

Spend time reviewing all of the different parts of you and add them to your chart. Regardless of your approval or disapproval, the results should be all inclusive. The more you identify the more developed your awareness.

10. *Exercise*: Write the answers to these questions in your journal to the best of your ability to help you identify significant parts within you:

How did your siblings treat you?

Did your older brother or sister like you? If not what did s/he say to you? What names did he or she call you? Any names they gave you, i.e., stupid, pest, brat, spoiled, etc. should be identified on your chart as roles. Older siblings are normally very angry at younger siblings just for being born and taking attention away from them. Again, this is not healthy but very normal. (assigned roles) Note any assigned roles or feelings you experienced as you were growing.

With adult siblings: Do you fight today? What do you fight about? How do you feel now when you fight or quarrel? What names do they call you today? Do they respect your opinion? (feelings) Describe how you feel as you answer the questions.

With family: Did you feel confused or sad by their treatment when you were a child or still today as an adult? Do they respect you today? Did they as a child? (feelings) How do you feel when you leave their house or they leave yours?

- Did you feel liked? (feelings)
- Were you jealous of them? Were they jealous of you? (feelings)
- Were you the favorite, or did you feel second to any of the others? (roles)
- Have you ever felt insecure? (feelings)
- Did you try to please your parents? (roles)
- Did you succeed or fail? If you felt either, include it or both on your chart. (beliefs)
- Were you a good girl/boy? If so, write it on the chart. (roles)
- Were you told not to cry, to be a big girl/boy? (roles)
- Did you ever become angry with your parents? If so, why? (feelings)
- What did you do and how did you react when you were angry? (feelings)
- How were you treated when you showed anger? (Role or feeling)
- Did you ever feel different or not good enough? (feelings)
- Did anyone ever tell you they were disappointed in you? How did that feel?
- Were you afraid to show your anger? (fear-feeling)
- Were you able to confront anger or did you withdraw? Rebel or people pleaser. (roles)
- Did anyone ever tell you that you were a

disappointment? If so, write disappointment and/or ashamed in your chart. (beliefs)

Today when you visit your parents, what are your feelings during the visit and after you leave their house?

The answers to these questions will give you additional ICs to include. For instance, if any of your siblings resented you, then you probably felt confused, unloved, or other distressing feelings. Identify all that have been experienced in your past or present. Remember your chart must identify feelings/emotions, roles you chose or roles you were given, and beliefs you have about yourself or beliefs others have about you. All of these feelings create your chart. Take heart, you are almost done with your chart, and it will be a tool you can use in all aspects of your life.

Additionally, it should be noted that the birth order of children in a family has a substantial impact on characteristics of a child. Birth order is significant in children developing familial roles. If you were the firstborn, your behavior and the role you play is generally very different from that of a middle child or last child. You might consider checking the Internet or buying a book on the birth order of children and its impact. It could be very enlightening. Rank in the family plays a significant role quite naturally without any awareness within the family. For example, first or only children are often "super achievers" while middle children can be "lost children," because they feel that they play an unimportant role in the family. The last child is always "the baby," and that could assume a number of implications within the family dynamics. It is a complex subject and deserves attention.

Please remember before tackling the next task requested of you that you need not be overwhelmed when you look at your completed chart and that you are not alone. Remember what I said earlier that one hundred percent of the charts developed in my practice look just like yours or the Universal List of Emotions/feelings, Roles and Beliefs. So after completing your list, slowly study every feeling from the list of identified children on your chart. If you have a friend who is also doing this process, share your charts with each other. When you observe the "normal" negativity you carry, it is a powerful message. Can you see the multitude of feelings that began when you were a child? Can you imagine how someone with all this "conflicting stuff" feels? Can you conceive how this person would view herself/himself and how difficult it would be to see a situation clearly? What kind of a day might they experience? Is it any wonder that many of us are confused or angry or scared of life? It is critical that you observe how these feelings/emotions/thoughts are damaging your health every day. The good news is that your awareness of the existence of this negativity makes it possible for you to transform your feelings into a more positive, healthy you.

When you are self-critical or make negative assertions about yourself, for example, statements such as I hate my hair, I hate my body, or I am too fat, you are doing severe damage to the cells of your body. Self criticism is usually harsher than disparagement by an enemy and rejection of self is the most destructive. Recognition and ownership of every thought, emotion, and belief within you, without guilt, judgment, or criticism, allows you to expand your awareness. Any feeling you expose is neither good nor bad, it just increases your ability to help yourself. Buddhists say, "What you resist persists," so don't resist just persist in your transformation.

Be aware of your thoughts and accept every part of you by allowing and welcoming each element without judgment. This process is about exposing every belief and feeling within you to you. Once recognized, it is possible for you to change your choices of thoughts and beliefs that are preventing your happiness in life. It is the letting go of the old and bringing in new thoughts and ideas. This is the divine path to freedom. It is your first and significant step toward unconditional self-love and a monumental part of your happiness and freedom from pain.

Importantly, remember that most of us experience softer feelings before we feel anger. It's easy to identify anger, but we are generally unaware of the hurt, sadness, disappointment, not good enough, not respected, unloved, victim, afraid, "chewed upon" feelings and others preceding the anger. It's fundamentally necessary to identify the feelings that caused the anger and include them in your chart, i.e., see the Universal Children Chart.

Distinguishing the softer feelings benefits your understanding of why you react excessively or dramatize at times, increasing your adrenaline level and creating havoc in your body. Many of us who have had repressed anger for years may experience depression, insecurity, or anxiety, but nevertheless it is anger deeply buried, and affecting your immune system and your health. Children remember everything they hear or experience consciously or subconsciously and carry it with them into adulthood. Ideas or statements you repeatedly hear eventually become what you accept as true.

Caution: If creating your personal chart of your inner children brings you deep emotions or feelings that create sadness, depression, or strong anxiety, we strongly advise that you find a therapist/psychologist or doctor immediately to help you with the process and the feelings. While this process may be somewhat distressing, sometimes it is simply too painful to face alone. It may reveal feelings that have been buried for years. So if you feel sad or down, let the process go until you see a professional therapist. The help of a professional therapist will guide you through the process while teaching you constructive coping mechanisms. If it is too painful, call your personal doctor immediately and ask for a referral to a clinic or individual therapist. Seek the help that you deserve.

In review, the task of creating your personal chart should include all that you have identified from your lists and reflect your answers to the questions asked in earlier steps. The *feelings and emotions* identified from childhood should be noted in the circles. Remember to identify the softer feelings that come before anger, irritation, disappointment, and resentment, for example: sad hurt, second best, not respected, etc. Those softer feelings always precede anger. The anger, despite its intensity, always follows hurt, sadness, not respected, etc. As you recognize your positive aspects add those to your circles too. Refer to the Universal Children Chart and Universal Children List for assistance in filling out your circles.

Again in review, list all of the *beliefs* you have about yourself and the beliefs others have about you and fill in more circles. Be as inclusive as you can. Beliefs include super-responsible, irresponsible, intelligent, stupid, not cool, selfish, not interesting, faithful, trusting, non-trusting, loving, cold, talented, not talented, etc. Use the Universal List to help identify labels that others have given you and that you have given to yourself. For example, "You are stupid." Or "I am fat."

Next list the *roles* you have chosen to live and the roles others have chosen for you, roles such as the critic, judge, good girl/boy, bad girl/boy, overachiever, underachiever, fixer, perfectionist, tomboy, bitch, protector, geek, and controller, or cowboy. Again, see Universal List and Universal Chart of Children. Upon completion, your personal chart should contain a minimum of forty to sixty inner children. Additional ones may be added in the borders. One page is normally inadequate to list everything you discover. Can you understand why you sometimes feel confused, why you might feel depressed, angry, hurt, or controlled? Are you able to comprehend why you might feel anger, rage, or depression? Do you appreciate why you are unable to hear your inner wisdom or your soul whispering to you?

You are now ready to move on. You may continue to add children to your chart as you identify them. Your chart is a permanent document that you can use and add to in the future if you choose.

Step Six

Your Inner Rascals Are Rattling Your Cage!

Myth: We make decisions from our objective, mature adult self.

Truth: Your decisions and your perceptions made by different, conflicting, reactive childhood beliefs are creating your behavior.

> *"The only limit to your realization of tomorrow will be your doubts of today."*
>
> Franklin D. Roosevelt

⌘ Activity: This step helps you scrutinize and detect how your thoughts are created and recognize how your daily perceptions affect your life. Your feelings influence your perceptions and your perceptions influence your feelings. Therefore together they affect every area of your life. This step increases your ability to see where the feelings originate and how your thoughts and perceptions create your actions influencing your life today.

Step 6: *The following exercise is crucial to identifying how your ICs affect your life today.* Review your journal and identify the documented experiences or situations that disturbed your peace and joy. With each experience, refer back to your personal chart and identify which inner children (ICs) created the problems. Log the IC's recognized from each experience into your journal. Matching your ICs with the disturbances in your life demonstrates how you make decisions in your life based on your inner children. This will verify you have been living your life through the emotional lens of a child. With your new awareness you have the power to make future decisions based on the wisdom of your soul or higher power.

As you read, notice which ICs of yours are the most active or common. You'll discover how your ICs affect your life all day, every day. Every argument in which you participate is created by your ICs. Every problem you ever had was exaggerated by your ICs. They continue to affect your life until you learn who they are and give them the security and love they need.

Who was the boss?

You (and the rest of us) have a flock of two to fifteen-year-olds determining your actions. They need your attention, and they need to be loved. If you learn how to appease them now, life will be smoother and more fun.

Know that every time you're not in peace and joy, your ICs are active and directing your life.

When your inner children are in conflict, they influence your decisions and actions. *The fun IC wants to go play, but the guilty, responsible IC says you should do your housecleaning.* The creative IC says *I want to be creative and paint, but the insecure IC says you're not good enough.* Daily, you struggle with different parts within you wanting a different outcome or action. One tired IC might want to relax but another super responsible IC says you *need* to get the chores done. A struggle ensues because if you relax, you feel guilty that you're "wasting time," and if you choose to do the chores, you feel resentful that you are obligated or expected to do them. Frequently, you are in a no-win situation with yourself. Always look to your ICs for the cause and then find the guilty party.

Did you ever try to lose weight and then eat ice cream or a brownie? You're disappointed in yourself and feel weak if you allow yourself to have the treat and feel disappointed and denied if you don't. Look for the guilty IC perpetrator and do your work. Talk to the guilty party nicely but firmly, and tell him/her that you need a break and have

What is going through this child's mind?

the brownie. Moderation is always the key. One smoker IC wants a cigarette and another guilty IC says, *No, you shouldn't.* Again, recognize the cause, talk to the ICs, and then make your own adult decision. The ICs nag and irritate and pester as they were taught through your childhood. Someone asks a favor of you and the people pleaser IC says, "Yes, I will do it," but the laid back or tired IC says, "Why did you say yes? That's the last thing I want to do today." There's always a guilty party in your ICs having their way with you.

With the many hurt, bellowing, complaining, and shouting children inside of you, it's difficult to hear the whisper of God in your soul. Your greatest challenge to being a mature, objective, happy adult is when all of the ICs are speaking for you at the same time. You can't make an objective decision with all of the dialogue perpetuating doubt, hurt, and uncertainty inside your head. It originates and gains strength from birth until death unless you choose to recognize and respect your feelings. And the worst part is that we pass this delusion on to generation after generation. Study your chart and read through every offender on the list, and you will then understand why you are conflicted, sad, or depressed, why you respond or over react as you do, why you are angry, feel no respect, and why you are confused by others.

"You may have to fight a battle more than once to win it."
Margaret Thatcher

11. *Exercise*: Part 1. Think of any incident in the past week that disturbed your peace of mind. Any incident will do, whether someone angered you, insulted you, or just plain ignored you. Then take your focus off *your perceptions of what they did to you* and look at the culprits in your personal chart and identify as many parts as possible that were affected by the incident and document them in your journal. The more IC reprobates you identify, the more aware you become. Focus on your feelings not the incident. Whenever you are taken out of peace and joy, you are reacting from the emotional lens of your child or your children. Time spent on somebody else's action is a *reaction* and is a waste of your time. When your "blaming IC" is active then you are focused outside of yourself and you are forgetting about being aware of your own thoughts and choices.

You can't control the choices of others, but you can control your choices. Identify your ICs, talk to them, soothe them, and then you are more able to change your thoughts and your choices. Choose to forgive, release, and be happy. Release of any negative thought is healthy.

In the grand scheme of life, most events are insignificant, especially when and if you are dealing with a major life-threatening disease. The threat of disease puts your thoughts in the proper perspective quickly. And your offended ICs would really rather be happy. This exercise illustrates how your ICs impact your life today and you how you, even now, continue to see your life through the emotional lens of a child. Every emotion (IC) that you identified from the incident above, originated in your childhood decisions. It is an emotion or belief that was created in your upbringing and is still making decisions for your reactions today. Every time you feel hurt or angry, it is an (IC). It is an emotion that you experienced as a young child because you knew of no better way to understand and/or resolve the occurrences in your life.

11. *Exercise*: Part 2. Think of times when you had the following feelings and identify a situation that activated the dominant IC. After you have chosen the incident and have identified the related child or children in you, talk to your ICs in a loving way, and tell the offended ICs how you would like to handle the same situation next time it is offered. Learning how to talk to these children inside is easy. Visualize yourself at six or seven years of age, standing in front of you crying because she or he is hurt and frustrated by something someone said or did to them. Check in with the child. Ask the child how he/she is feeling and what hurt them. Then talk to the child just as you would if a real child was standing before you *because there is a real child listening* inside of you. As a parent to your IC's, visualize your six-year-old child experiencing every feeling on this list and document any new insights:

    - frustrated
    - not good enough
    - out of control
    - hurt
    - anxious
    - sad
    - judged
    - critical
    - unloved
    - not lovable
    - not respected
    - not validated
    - like a failure
    - disappointed in her holiday
    - disappointed in someone
    - "bad"

- uncomfortable
- criticized
- not liked
- unwanted
- tense
- anxious

Each incident where you identify any of the above emotions within you, your ICs are actively dominating your feelings and the situation. Your inner children are active anytime that you are not feeling peaceful. As you identify those occasions, document the feelings and the reason for the lack of peace in your journal. As time passes and you continue this process, you can read older parts of your journal and see the progress that you are making in your life. You can witness how proficient you are becoming at identifying and pacifying your ICS.

Our inner children are not all active at one time. They appear to come and go, but they are always present within and ready to react. They can be inappropriate and destructive and when angry, act out, creating problems for you. The old saying, "Don't bite off your nose to spite your face," seems appropriate here. We, even as adults, make decisions that we know are not in our best interests.

We often feel foolish and remorseful after acting out from the rascals because our ICs can help us or hurt us. They are the foundation of what many call "the ego." When you say, "I don't know what got into me," it is one of your inner children. Remember that the little troublemakers sometimes react in your best interest and other times not. They (and you when they take over) are children and don't know any better. They don't always make good decisions. It is important to remember that they can only speak *for* you when you are *unaware* of them. It behooves you to get to know them well and love them and raise them with the love that they and you deserve.

The more you write in your journal and practice this exercise whenever you are not in peace and joy, the quicker you will progress in this process and the sooner you will find peace.

Having your IC family within is not just your problem and common only to you. The other person who just hurt you or insulted you also has a family of kids within! Consult your chart again, and recognize the guilty parties of the other person, who were acting or reacting for them, and you will see the other person's IC family. Review the universal chart of IC's earlier in this book for assistance. You will have a whole new perspective and you might even feel sorry for them. Their kids may be more active than yours.

The following ICs can and will make troublesome decisions for you, too, so be aware of when you are taking on any of the roles listed below.

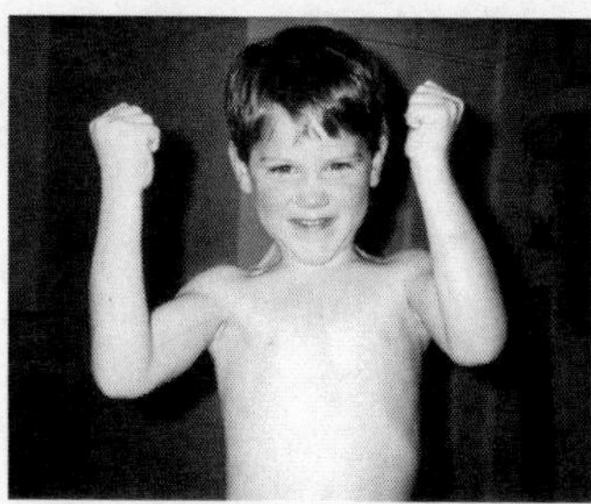

How would you describe this boy?

- The perfectionist
- The critic
- The judgmental one
- The controller
- The rascal

- The anxious one
- The angry one
- Not respected
- Disappointed
- Frustrated
- Invaded
- Intolerant, etc.

How would you describe this girl?

The most significant insight for me was that although everybody appeared different, I and each of my clients and my friends listed the same feelings, roles, and beliefs on their charts. I've taught people of all ages, all levels of education, different sexual preferences, all nationalities, and people from janitors to CEOs, and they all had similar kids with minor differences. The basic feelings are the same in all charts. As a result, I developed the Universal Chart. Everyone has their insecurities, hurts, sadness, fears, betrayal, not good enough, failure, not loved, unlovable (these last two are different and feel different) despite their differences in life style. Until I discovered this fact, I always felt different and alone in my feelings. I finally realized that what I felt was also common in all.

Once you are aware of how your ICs influence your life, you proceed to the next step and begin communicating with them and help them see the situation from your soul or Higher Self. You are going to love them and raise them to maturity. Then the fun starts. Insecurity arises when the ICs are in conflict; confidence can only exist with the awareness and the integration of the many personalities within.

Additionally, you will have the benefit of responding differently to others when you recognize their IC's if their behavior irritates you or creates problems for you. Their ICs will be very apparent to you, making it easier to deal with problems and personalities.

> *"Joy, rather than happiness, is the goal of life, for joy is the emotion which accompanies our fulfilling our nature as human beings. It is based on the experience of one's identity as a being of worth and dignity."*
>
> Rollo May, PhD, Author

Step Seven

Love and Talk to Your Inner Children

⌘ *Activity: Learn how to talk to your ICs and love yourself—all of you!*

Step 7: In this step, you initiate communication with your ICs, recognize their needs (actually your needs), and teach them how to love you. The goal is to heal your ICs and integrate them into a more harmonious group made whole. They are part of your total, and they need never to be criticized or judged again. They might need to be taught how to respond differently but they need to be taught with love and respect. You, the adult, especially need self-love and respect because you are the whole of the group. You alone are affected by the conflict within.

After years of living with my neediest IC troublemakers (the guilty one and the people pleaser), I, Ali, discovered the reason I was on this earth (a question I asked of you in chapter five). My personal answer is and always will be: *I am on this earth to learn how to respect myself, love myself, forgive myself, and honor my needs finally and unconditionally and then offer that same unconditional love, respect and forgiveness to all others.* By doing so, I am at long last honoring the God within me and able to accept God's love. I irrevocably give myself permission to make myself happy despite creating anger or disappointment in another. (More on God in a later chapter, so please don't take this time to be offended if the term "God" disturbs you. There is additional info later on for you to choose or reject.)

This discovery and choice to take care of myself first before others was and still is difficult for the people pleaser in me and in the beginning of the process it is also an outrageous assertion to most clients. But by the time they have practiced the process and witnessed the results within themselves and others, they are much more accepting and convinced this is the healthier and happier long term approach.

Somehow, our conditioning to help and please others has led us to believe that our own needs should be secondary, with women especially. The fact remains that you are the only one who can make yourself happy. No other can consistently bring happiness to you except you. The answer to why you are here in this body and this life is to give yourself (and the Higher Power or Wisdom within you) unconditional love and acceptance. Please suspend disbelief here. When you read further, you will understand why this is the bigger picture and the number one reason for life.

When asked their reason for living, clients if they have an answer, consistently answer, "I am here to help others." This reason is flawed because no one can constantly give anyone outside themselves happiness. Happiness comes from within. And it is impossible to help others on a consistent basis until you realize self-love. Even with well developed self-love, you nevertheless cannot decide or influence how another person should or will feel. Every human being has free will just as you do. Only they can decide how they choose to feel. Happiness is an inside job. Your focus must always be on making yourself happy. If you choose to be responsible for your own happiness then you can at other times choose to put another first. But if that is your choice, then at least you must realize that you are choosing to put another being first.

We must learn how to change our thoughts and perceptions before we can lead a joyful, healthy life. It is critical that you meet your own needs with unconditional love regardless of what others think. *Only we can make ourselves happy and respond to our needs all of the time.* Remember Dr Siegel's words,

> *"Self-love and self-esteem are required. We must start with self-love and self-healing in order to be able to extend it to others."* John Steinbeck said, *"If we could learn to like ourselves, even a little, maybe our cruelties and angers might melt away."*

Unconditional love for that special, unique person you are is *your number one reason for walking this earth.* The reason you must develop self-love first is because without unconditional love for self, you cannot provide unconditional love consistently to anyone else. *And your second reason for being here* is to give unconditional love to everyone else, without exception.

When you have fulfilled your own needs, it is easy to love others without resentment. Consistent sacrifice will in time, create resentment, fatigue, and illness within you.

Pearl S. Buck was wise enough to say, *"To serve is beautiful, but only if it is done with joy and a whole heart."*

You can't have a whole heart and serve others when you do not possess self-love. And you cannot serve others by neglecting your own truth and your own needs. No one can take care of you as well as you can, because no one is with you 100 percent of the time.

Wayne Dyer says, *"You can not give away what you do not possess. You can't make lemonade from apples. You have to own an apple to give an apple."* That's why it is *vital* to develop self-love first. Only with self-love can you give unconditionally to others. If you are feeling resentment, guilt, anger, sadness, and negativity, then you are not taking care of your own needs. You are the best and only person for the job, so don't neglect yourself and put yourself first! The only kind of love that you want for yourself and others is unconditional. Pure love cannot exist with conditions. God is pure love and as God's child so are you. So it makes sense that it is essential to learn to be happy with yourself before you can help anyone else to happiness.

The importance of unconditional self-love is indisputably vital. Self-love is crucial to healing and living a life of purpose. We have been conditioned from childhood to struggle and make others happy. From birth on, ninety-eight percent of us have been led, manipulated, controlled, and taught to do as we are told. We are taught that selfish is "bad." So we grow up with a setup for failure. The only way to happiness is to look inward, forgive your self for not being perfect, and develop self-love to heal all of the hurts from childhood. Love is about discovering a potential joy—a potential that already exists but is buried beneath a pile of ICs, fears, worries, doubt, and self-abuse.

We fantasize about love. We think we will fall in love and make each other happy. We actually *expect* others to make us happy and we believe we are able to make others happy. Now that you are familiar with all of the unhappy culprits and rascals within you and believe they exist within everyone else, you can see that it is an inside job. Try as you might, you cannot make someone else secure when they have so many ICs active in their thinking, telling them that they are not good enough. Just as I am powerless to change my own beautiful granddaughters' minds about their own beauty and thinness, you are powerless to change others.

The virtual truth is that no one can make another happy consistently. Inevitably you will be disappointed by even the most well-meaning people because they are human. We must do it for ourselves because happiness is an inside job. When you choose to give someone the power to make you happy, then you also give them the ability to take that happiness away whenever they choose. Don't surrender your power and your joy to anyone. Feeling happy is a choice. It is your decision and your responsibility. Your job is to forgive yourself for being human and love yourself unconditionally in spite of not being perfect.

Sigmund Freud was a remarkable, wonderful man in so many ways. He and Einstein are my heroes. They had understanding, wisdom and insight well beyond their time. Freud said, *"Most people do not really want freedom, because freedom involves responsibility, and most people are frightened of responsibility."* This is true and for good reason. Taking responsibility for everything in your life is really tough and complicated. However, understanding your IC's does help.

The path to unconditional love includes loving all of your ICs no matter how unlovable they act. Embrace them and love them inclusively, for without your love, self-love cannot exist. How sad that the majority of us don't love ourselves—that we criticize most everything about us. When you embrace one part of you but reject and deny others, you are in effect judging yourself harshly and saying, "I love this part, but not that part." That is judgment, not unconditional love. This type of judgment is feeding your body's cells with negativity and chastisement. How fair is that to you because your inner child knows no better? You can teach that child the healthy way to feel.

This step of the process is the foundation for success. You can and will become the loving, forgiving parent that was not present or available when you were a child. Consult your chart in times of anger or negativity so you can recognize and identify your ICs/little rascals. Know and accept that they are real because they will always exist in your mind. This process is not about deleting every negative within because that is impossible. It is about learning how to recognize when they are involved with your decision making, and become skilled at managing them and loving them. To integrate the different ICs, you have to recognize which are active and then answer their needs by giving them acceptance and love. When you recognize negative, old conditioning and behavior, you talk yourself through old feelings and choose to release the negativity. You integrate the kids by talking to them, just like settling an argument between two fighting children. Life is about learning how to forgive your self for not being perfect and accepting and loving yourself anyhow.

Different issues developed in your life at a variety of ages, so the IC's are a range of diverse ages. Once familiar with them, you can almost feel the age of the child that is active. For some reason, many of mine were in the seven year-old and the twelve-year-old brackets. Anger develops when our needs are neglected or unmet, which tells you that anger begins early in life. Interestingly enough, my brother was born when I was seven. Until then I had been an only, cherished child with all of my parent's attention. When he was born, my mother's attention was focused on him. I probably was very angry and jealous at that time which is when and why many of my own IC's were born. Looking at pictures of yourself as a child will help you with your visualizations.

You must see and visualize this child as you are talking to them. If you find it difficult to know how to speak to your inner children then think about what you would say to your own children. I suggest you study a picture of yourself and then visualize that five-year-old standing in front of you crying because she/he feels hurt and alone and thinks no one likes her/him. She is lonely and sad and confused and feeling unloved. What would you say to that child who was just abandoned by her playmates and is sad and confused? What would you say to an eight year old boy who just lost his ball game for his teammates? How do you give a child reassurance? You would talk to your IC's the same way you would console a real child standing in front of you.

I suggest you sit down, put her on your lap, hug her and hold her tight, and tell her how cute she is, how much you love her, and how you are going to take good care of her and you are never going to let anyone hurt her again. If someone has hurt your little boy or rejected him, pick him up, put him on your lap, hug him, and tell him how much you love him. Tell him that if someone was mean to him that it is not about him, it is about the other child and give him the love and attention you would have liked to receive as a child. And tell him that you will protect him. Never deny him. That has happened too often to him. Love him or her unconditionally.

When I began this practice with one of my own inner children, I saw her as six or seven years of age, and she was lonely, afraid, sad, hurt, and confused. After holding her on my lap, I would tell her she was the most beautiful little girl in the world, I loved her, she was wonderful, and I was not going to let anyone hurt her again. Every time I felt sad or hurt or out of peace and joy, I repeated the identical sentences over and over to myself and to her. It took about two years before she (my hurt little girl) trusted me and felt better and then the feelings began to dissipate. Today I cannot remember when I have felt hurt or sad. Those feelings are no longer real to me. I realize that others have those feelings and therefore can be hurtful, but I am not affected by them any longer. My little girl has finally grown up without guilt for saying no or taking care of herself.

Interestingly enough, in the beginning, I could almost see her looking at me and thinking, "*Yeah, you were the meanest of all to me and you want me to trust you?*" It will take time, but they will trust you if you are consistent. I recognized over time that my most active children were the "not respected" and "not good enough" little girls. In retrospect, when I reviewed my childhood, I realized I absolutely was not respected in any way. I had no power, no respect, and no choice in any matter. I was told what to do, and out of fear, I did it without a whimper. Not the healthiest way to raise a child as deep and passionate as I. It took years to reassure my kids that the only respect they needed was mine, and I was giving them respect gladly and deservedly. I taught them that "hurt people hurt people" and when someone was hurtful to me, it wasn't about me. It defined the person that was being hurtful. It didn't define me in any way.

Your goal is to liberate yourself from the guilt and all other destructive useless feelings. It is time to heal the hurts created by ignorance and pain by your self and others over the years. Our parents had no one to teach them, and we had no role model to show us how to deal with our feelings differently, but today you have the answer. You can now help yourself and assist others by example.

Our inner children are just different aspects of our personality. Some are stronger than others, just as our personality has more intense or passionate aspects. When I was helping Lynn Jones work with her ICs, she was determined to erase one she named Critical Woman from her chart. She wanted to remove her, rid herself of Critical Woman, which I believe is instinctual. She believed if she removed her, she was gone. She believed she, Critical Woman, would no longer bother her. Your ICs do not just go away. If they did, you would have no problems after age ten. They must be recognized, loved, guided, and allowed to grow just as any child would need.

I guided Lynn, my friend who wrote the foreword, to accept and love Critical woman (CW). CW was just one aspect of Lynn's personality that she had rejected and denied for years. She (that part of Lynn) needed love and acceptance, so I led her to give CW the love she wanted, helped her to recognize her good qualities and to call on CW when she needed her strength. Once recognized, Lynn had a great deal of work to do with CW because she did not like that critical aspect of her personality. That characteristic, CW, will not relax and change until Lynn can recognize, accept, respect, and demonstrate that she loves her. We actually do not want her (Lynn's) strength to go away. CW needs to feel loved and join the rest of the healthy parts. She may return again, but if forgiven for not being perfect, given the love and respect needed and knows she is loved, she will continue to respond to loving kindness, and provide Lynn with strength and growth.

Most of our inner children are not as complicated as CW. CW was an important fraction of Lynn and dealing with that aspect of her personality was a significant one. CW or CG (Critical Guy) exists in all of us, and all ICs are just aspects of the whole and our ego personality. They are personality aspects. They are active and can cause problems for you. Recognizing them, learning to deal with the different aspects, and giving each of them what you need within, helps you gain control of your life and makes life manageable. It is never too late to learn to love yourself. It just takes time and practice after you become aware of all that is within you.

Loving and learning to communicate with your inner

children requires vigilance and persistent awareness of your feelings and thoughts. Sounds demanding and it is at first, but after time it becomes second nature, and a healthy habit. Several years ago, I read in A Course in Miracles, that I must always be *vigilant* in my thoughts; my initial reaction was that it seemed harsh and unnecessary. Over time, however, I not only realized the importance of that fundamental statement, but that it was a prerequisite to getting well and feeling better about myself.

Anthony De Mello, Jesuit priest and author, says that learning to observe yourself is vital to joy and health. He explains that *"'I,' the higher self, observes 'me,' the ego or personality. You observe not to condemn but to understand yourself. By observing, you are more likely to be able to embrace all of what you feel and begin to create yourself and a life you choose."*

Observing yourself through your ICs becomes easier and more meaningful when you are aware of them and recognize which are active when problems occur. This knowledge gives you power and the ability to speak to them, teach them, respect all parts, and transform them into the whole person you hope to be in your lifetime. Continue to journal daily, and as you recognize more of your personality and include them in your list for your personal chart.

12. *Exercise*: Find a few pictures of yourself as a child at different ages.

A typical picture to remind you of your childhood.

Start with pictures of when you were two, four, seven or eight, eleven or twelve, and as a teenager. Place these pictures in different rooms of your house so that they are present in your life—on the refrigerator, bathroom mirror, bedside table, in your purse or pocket, and wherever you spend time. Use the picture as a bookmark for your journal, hang it next to your computer, on the visor of your car, or on the coffee table where you watch TV. If you have no pictures of yourself as a child, find some cute little kids in magazines and adopt them as yours.

Identify the most predominant five or six ICs in your chart and give them names. You can use descriptive names like "Miss Insecure" or "Master Stubborn," "My Little

Victim" or "Angry One," "Critical Joe" or "Dark Daisy." Or you can use nicknames like "Lucky" or "Plucky" or "Guilty Girl or Guy." It doesn't matter what you name them, as long as the name means something to you. Giving your ICs a name makes it easier to communicate with all of the different parts within you. When you become aware of the presence of "Miss Insecure," you might say to her, "Okay. I hear you. I know you are scared, but I want you to know it will be okay. I will take care of you." When "Critical Joe" is present, you might say, "Not now, Critical Joe." But always go back and give little Joey the love and respect he deserves.

Ask questions like, "What is the most important thought for me to focus on now?" or "Who would I be if I had nothing to fear?" Remember Francis Bacon's quote,

"A prudent question is one half of wisdom."

Answer the question and then talk to that inquisitive or fearful child. Visualize picking him/her up and holding him/her close and saying "I love you." Hold the picture close and place it over your heart, and tell that little one, "You are wonderful. You are safe. I will not let anyone ever hurt you again." Then say, "You are wonderful. You are so cool. You are simply wonderful." Say anything that you would want said to you today. Just be loving, accepting, and respectful of his/her feelings. This child might be doubtful that she/he can believe you since you have not always been protective of her or him. She might not believe you, but she will if you are consistently giving her love when she acts out.

When you feel hurt or angry, go to the picture and give

the little child love as you would any five or six or seven year old in distress. Look into the child's eyes. What do you see there? Then listen carefully. You might experience this little child in the picture giving you messages, too. Hear the little voice telling you exactly what is so troubling. Ask the child questions. Then sit quietly and listen to what comes to you.

As you sit quietly with the picture of you the child, you have taken the first step in communicating with your ICs. You are also beginning to observe yourself. How do you feel? What are you thinking? Are you feeling foolish? I did at first, but the more I practiced, the more relief I felt as an adult.

Give it a try! Your inner selves will come alive and you will find yourself having amazing, colorful and meaningful conversations with the wisdom within you, making exciting discoveries about yourself.

Look at the chart you have created, and congratulate your self because you should be highly applauded and pleased. It is an amazing achievement. By writing in your journal, you were able to create your chart and you are well on your way to awareness, health, freedom, and abundance. You are ready to reap the rewards. Congratulations.

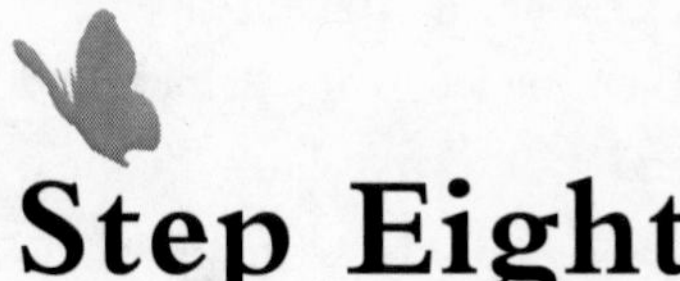

Step Eight

Change How You See Your Life

Mirror, Mirror on the Wall

Myth: You are powerless over your mind and the life and health you have created.

Truth: You are very powerful and have created your life as you know it. Because of that, you can look in the mirror without judgment and change the way you see yourself and your life thereby creating the moments, the days, and the years as you wish them to be.

⌘ Activity VIII: Learning how to change your views of your inner world, the outside world and other people's actions by making different choices in your perceptions, your choices and your observations of all three.

Step 8: Hopefully completing your chart has given you a

greater understanding of your previously undiscovered self. Now that you are aware of your ICs, you can proactively choose your reactions/responses by changing your thoughts to take control and be proactive in the future. You are responsible for your choices. You can change your life. You are capable of being as happy as you desire when you let go of judgment and blame and focus on yourself and your own feelings. Blaming others for any anger you feel is projection and a distraction. People will always give you opportunities to blame them with their words and actions, but every time you fall into judgment and blame another person, you waste time; your precious time, not theirs, and your valued life, not theirs.

Mirror, mirror, on the wall! Tell me what you see! It is not what the mirror sees; rather what do you see and feel when you look into your thoughts? The goal of this step is to apply your expanded knowledge and awareness to become conscious of your judgment and your blame of others. Remember, you can change your thinking and make different choices, but others have the right to choose their own way as well. Since you cannot consistently change anything but your mind, focus on yourself, use the power of your mind, and choose another path. When you recognize you are judging yourself or others, decide differently and release the negativity. Decide on peace instead of blame. Appreciate your lesson and choose to see that others are perfect teachers for you to practice your new thinking.

To realize this goal, it is essential to modify your views. When interacting with others, unless it involves violence, destruction, or harm to someone, every person has the right to make his or her own choices. Of course there are exceptions to this statement but basically if two people cannot agree on a compromise, your choice is to respect their decision, or choose to leave the situation. In friendships, partnerships, and marriage, one can never consistently control the actions, feelings or desires of the other person. Often I find when counseling couples, that one partner always wants the other to change and sees no need for change in themselves. Compromise should always be a two way street. When both people give a little, real change is not only possible but probable. Relationships of any kind are *always opportunities* to learn and become more conscious of your choices.

Stuart Wilde, a well known author and speaker, says that your neighbors' opinion of you is none of your business. As a recovering people pleaser I have learned to agree with him. What others say or do is *not* your business. What *you* say and do *is* your business. Making changes in your thinking about yourself and others is simple but not easy. Your thought system has been habitual for a long time. With time and practice, it is possible and your payoff is happiness and freedom.

> *"Freedom is man's capacity to take a hand in his own development. It is our capacity to mold ourselves."*
>
> Dr. Rollo May

Why are so many of us unhappy? There will always be occasions when life presents lessons in the form of hardships, losses, illness, death of loved ones and other difficult situations that we do not always understand. These situations, though they present challenges and trying times, are also opportunities to learn and grow. There is no argument that life presents harsh occurrences at times. We will all endure loss, death of loved ones, illness and adversity. However, often times, we are unhappy because we blame others and offensively or defensively accuse them inappropriately. This choice of response only serves to initiate additional inappropriate behavior on both sides of the issue. You feel hurt and blame the behavior of the other person. It is easier to blame others than to look within and seek resolution internally. I, too, was unaware of my own defensiveness. In the past, when someone accused me of being defensive, I would defend and say, "I'm just explaining myself." I was not aware that my need to "explain" my action was a defensive response. I, who worked in the psychiatric/mental health field for years, did not recognize my own defensiveness.

In instances such as divorce, separation, and other divisive situations, the other person doesn't need to understand your motivation. Only you need to understand your intention and your purpose. When you understand and accept your reasons for your defensiveness and insecurities then no one else need understand. It isn't necessary because you can choose to forgive you for not being perfect, release any blame and move on. This choice eventually brings real happiness.

Examples of "blaming statements" are:

- You made me feel bad. (blaming victim)
- You're acting like a child! (judgmental)
- You're too sensitive! Or, you are insensitive. (judgmental)
- What did I do now? (victim)
- What about me? (you are supposed to take care of you)

- You don't love me! (victim)
- You don't care about me! (victim)
- I hate you! (judgmental)
- You hurt my feelings. (victim)
- You never (or always) _______. (judgmental and expectant)
- It's your entire fault! (blame)
- If you didn't have these problems, I would be okay. (blame and irresponsible)
- You need to take care of me. (victim)
- You don't answer my needs. (accusatory victim)
- You're selfish! (judgmental)
- You make me feel sad. (victim and judgmental)

The above are blaming statements and often indicate neediness and a victim attitude that originated in childhood when you actually *were* a victim. In adulthood however, accusing others of hurting your feelings eliminates your responsibility for your choice of feelings and places that responsibility on the other person. It speaks volumes about your life experience. Behavior that worked against you when you were a child doesn't usually work any better in adulthood. And blaming others forces you to remain powerless in the victim role. You have no power because you gave it all away, without awareness. I recommend that you cease to blame others, take responsibility for your thoughts and actions and reclaim your power. It feels better in the long run. Eleanor Roosevelt said,

"No one can make you feel inferior without your consent."

How often do you hear accusatory statements made to you

and how often do you fault others? Answer these questions in your journal. Then write your response to the question, "What is the most loving thing I could say or do now?"

To thine own self be true. Be honest with yourself. Blaming creates disharmony, especially in you. It makes you angry, judgmental, and powerless. The tendency to accuse others can be changed, but only if you choose to take your power back, look within and examine your thoughts and feelings. It's not fun being a victim. Being in charge of your emotions is strong and impressive. With awareness, you can consistently and powerfully be in charge of your beliefs and thoughts.

Question: What prevents you from realizing your potential?

Answer: Focusing on others and blaming them for the problem—faulting others for your problems. When you blame others, you're a victim, and once a victim you are helpless. Then you are lost in your ICs.

"You hurt me." No one can hurt your feelings unless you allow them. Anyone can make hurtful comments, but only you can choose to be offended by them. Accusatory statements reflect more about the person speaking them than they do about the person to whom they are directed. Unless someone physically harms you, they cannot hurt you. We have been taught to believe that when people say cruel words, we can take them personally and feel hurt, sad, etc. False! No one has the power to hurt you by words or accusations unless you allow it. In a German concentration camp, Viktor Frankl refused to allow the Nazis to dominate him. He said,

> *"Everything can be taken from a man but one thing; the*

> *last of the human freedoms–to choose one's attitude in any given set of circumstances, to choose one's own way."*

Hurt people hurt other people. Hurt is passed to the next generation without awareness. Happy and contented people do not say harmful things or perform unkind acts to others. They don't need to. Wounded individuals are driven to feel better, and erroneously think if they put others down they will feel superior.

> *"If you are distressed by anything external, the pain is not due to the thing itself. But to your estimate of it, and this you have the power to revoke at any moment."*
>
> Mark Aurelius Antonius

When you choose to feel attacked by a person's words or accusations, your immediate response is usually a need to defend yourself. In defending yourself, you attack back. When you attack back, the other will defend and feel a need to attack again. By that time, there is no control in either of you and the problem escalates. The ICs attack, defend, attack back, defend back. One of you has to stop, walk away, choose not to take it personally, and stop defending. It is a vicious circle that can only be broken by disregarding any attack on your character. Think Jesus. Jesus never defended himself and was silent when accused. Silence often stops the argument and the problem can be handled after the anger and hurt has passed. Only then can it be resolved. If silence provokes violence, leave immediately.

I believe everyone does the best they can under the circumstances in which they live. We've never been taught all the rules of how to respond in a more productive way when we are angry and hurt or we would! The Golden Rule says, "*Do unto others as you would have them do to you.*" Well, we do! Reversed, since we are already critical of ourselves we are also critical of others, oftentimes without even knowing the people involved. We pass judgment on ones' clothes, looks, weight, actions, level of sophistication, etc. just as we judge the same qualities in ourselves. Most of this happens without any awareness that we are judging. Unfortunately as you see others, you see yourself and as you judge others you judge others you judge yourself. So let's be kinder to ourselves so we can be sympathetic to others.

Is your present behavior working for you? Dr. Phil, a well known, popular TV personality, frequently asks his guests, "How is this behavior working for you?" Most of the time it doesn't! When you ignore problems or anger, they do not disappear. They gather strength and go underground in your body and get stored as anxiety. If your tendency leans toward an explosive type person, hurt and fear accumulate in your body and erupt as anger and anxiety when someone irritates or disappoints you. Unresolved problems don't resolve themselves. They remain and accumulate enough stress in the body to create disease especially as we get older. Our bodies talk to us constantly. We don't usually listen until it debilitates us.

Choices and thoughts can be perplexing. The origin of your thoughts many times may be unknown or undiscovered even by yourself. Isn't it frightening or disconcerting that most of us live our lives, taking actions based upon decisions and beliefs born of a thought that perhaps has been ingrained in our being for so long that even we don't know its true origin, let alone whether or not that thought serves us. Confusing isn't it?

13. *Exercise*: Do any of the following apply to you? Again, journal on any part to which you relate.

    - Do you ever feel confused or regret about your reaction or others comments?
    - Do you ever feel self-hatred or criticize yourself?
    - Do you ever use self-sabotaging and self-destructive behavior?
    - Do you have an inability to have a fulfilling or lasting relationship?
    - Do you have a fear of intimacy?
    - Do you have frequent arguments and misunderstandings with family, friends, or coworkers?
    - Have you been divorced?
    - Do you have frequent illness?
    - Do you fear of change, failure, the future?
    - Do you feel disappointment or disillusionment?
    - Do you have low self-esteem or feel insecure?

All of the above problems are considered typical and in fact are normal to experience, but they don't have to be present in your life. Listening to your ICs is like listening to a different channel that blocks you from hearing the channel of your inner wisdom. Your fear and your constant inner critic prevent you from experiencing the divine within you. Anthony De Mello wrote,

> *"The secret is that everything is as good or as bad as one's opinion makes it."*

Life is not about saving others at your expense; it is about saving yourself and then helping others from a healthier unconditional love. Otherwise yours is an unfulfilled life.

14. *Exercise*: Questions to ponder and answer in your journal: Document your answers to the following questions in your journal. Take several days to answer these questions. I suggest you answer one or two questions per day. Add any newly identified inner children to your personal chart.

    - What has caused your unhappiness in the past?
    - What are the disappointments in your life? Describe them.
    - What are your successes? Describe them.
    - What behaviors of yours hinder your potential?
    - Why are the obstructions there? Did anyone tell you that you could not pursue your dreams or follow your passion?
    - Have you created a self-fulfilling prophecy for yourself? Describe any you recognize. What phrases do you use to describe yourself repeatedly?
    - What would you like to do differently?
    - What will it take for you to create life differently?
    - What do you see as your ideal life?
    - What would it take to achieve your goals?
    - What is the most important focus for you now?
    - What are your top four goals?

It is a remarkable accomplishment to reach this point and your well thought out answers give you a blueprint for your future. Reread your answers and identify the steps you must take and want to take to achieve your top four goals. Write small steps with timeframes for your goals. Decide what you want to accomplish and start working on the first steps today. Examples follow.

Here are example of answers to above questions and goals as a result of the insight.

My anger, judging others and judging my self have all caused much unhappiness in my past. Sometimes I react and get angry or blow up quickly and then am sorry afterwards, but it is too late. I would like to be successful, but I speak without thinking and that gets me in trouble. I would like to think before I speak. My anger and impatience to speak creates problems for me. When I am angry, my goal for the future is to stop and listen and think the situation through until the anger has passed and then try to handle the situation calmly and speak my truth. I will plan ahead. I will also listen to the other person's point of view for any truth and try to find a compromise. I will validate the other person's feelings by understanding their feelings even if I do not agree with them.

Sometimes I am afraid that I can't do a good job, so I don't even try to do well. I am afraid of failing and that people will think me stupid or silly so I don't give my opinions. Sometimes I do not ask questions in groups because I fear they are stupid questions. I can see that my fear prevents me from doing things I really want to do. Goal: I will recognize and work on my fear and try new things. I will ask questions so I can have the answers. No question is stupid. If I am afraid of what others think, I will remind me that this is my life and I can do what I want. I will try ________ (whatever you might have been afraid of doing in the past (for example dancing in public or sharing your ideas in public).

How do you change your perceptions?

"We experience what we believe. You most likely believe that

> *your experiences have taught you what is real and what is true—at least for you. However, what you may not know is that your beliefs—conscious or unconscious—determine what you experience. "Experiences do not determine what you believe. What you first of all believe is what you will experience. It follows then, that if you wish to experience life in new ways, you need to examine your belief systems. Change your consciousness and you'll change your life."*
>
> The Daily Guru.

The Daily Guru is a no cost daily motivational internet site, thedailyguru.com Richard Bach said, *"Sooner or later, those who win are those who think they can."* The real answer to any problem lies within you. Self-awareness helps you with change and gives reliable answers to why you feel and react as you do. Self-awareness is the key to making changes so to become better informed, observe yourself and be honest about your feelings, your choices, your behavior and learn from any mistakes. Awareness gives you power and wisdom and encourages you to be who you want to be. Know thyself. Take responsibility for your behavior, and capture the power to create your desire.

> *"If I have lost confidence in myself, I have the universe against me."*
>
> Ralph Waldo Emerson

Perception is simply a point of view or an opinion founded by your observations and over time forms the definition of what you believe you see in any given situation. Your perceptions create your thoughts, your thoughts create your beliefs, and your beliefs create your actions. Your actions create your life. Your perceptions, once formed, are based only on your personal belief, and can often produce a tendency for instant, impulsive action. Your perceptions created your IC's and your IC's often lead you to impulsive action. Impulsive actions often create chaos in your life. If we are to see differently, we need to filter our perceptions past our emotions and through the eyes of awareness. Perceptions and misperceptions create barriers and problems in your life. You can always choose to see differently. Your beliefs become your truth! Your perceptions or misperceptions become what you see. Don't rely on perceptions from your IC's alone to make your decisions. *A Course in Miracles* says you can choose to see peace in any situation. Choose wisely, it is your life.

A self-fulfilling prophecy is created by repetitive thoughts and words because your thoughts and beliefs are powerful. They create your reality, so be alert to the power of your words and thoughts. When you expose the emotions creating your responses, you change your perceptions and your options. Norman Vincent Peale said, *"Change your thoughts and you change your world."*

Ask which IC is making the best choice for you. We have free will and our choices create our life exactly as we choose. Choose to love your "inner kids" and have fun with them. Today, I think mine are comical and they make me laugh. My sense of humor has grown significantly over the years as I have released the pain and hurt from my earlier life. Because of that wonderful inner voice and its eternally forgiving advice, I can laugh at me when I am lost in them. Then I tell them how cute they are but they need to "give it up" and move on because the grown up in me knows what works for us. So the IC's never really "go away." They just mature and integrate the total YOU and allow peace to enter into your life.

We blame spouses, bosses, children, or jobs for our unhappiness. We think the problem is external. Happiness and unhappiness are always internal, never external. The external often does provide an opportunity for you to feel happy or unhappy and offers opportunities for you to learn and change the way you see your reality. There will always be someone to offend you or blame you or be offended by your words or actions. Start asking God or your higher self to help you to see each situation differently. Tell yourself you can choose to see it differently. Ask for guidance and you will receive it.

> *One would be in less danger from the wiles of the stranger*
> *if one's own kin were more fun to be with.*
> Ogden Nash, *Family Court in Hard Lines*

Begin by changing your relationship with your parents. As children, we had few choices but to do as we were told, and that is how our inner children developed. As offspring, most of us tended to see our parents as all-powerful. We wished or thought our mother could be more nurturing or our father could be more (or in my case less) protective. So we blame our parents, but no parents are perfect. They did and do the best they can. Parents are human, so it is inevitable that in some instances they will disappoint us and themselves. Disappointment is universal for humans so welcome it and decide who you want to be when it is your turn. As adults, however, we do need to understand that our parents did the best they could with the resources they had. They acted as they were taught by their parents. They were molded just as you were. They struggle with their own feelings of inadequacy and feelings of anger. They have ICs, too! Everybody on earth is doing the best they can. Let's find our freedom and let's withhold judgment. Each person is exactly as he or she should be to learn their lessons and to help you learn yours.

As parents, it's never too late to change your relationship with your adult children. Only you can change your life. No one can do it for you because it is *your* choices that you need to change to transform your life. That is why we cannot change our adult children's lives despite how much we may want to. They deserve respect in their choices and their decisions. They may ask our opinion, and then we are free to give it, but the final decision is theirs. Releasing the need to change others can be healing for you and for your children. It can be freedom.

Changing your life view requires you look at your relationships from a different perspective, especially with your partner. You expect that if she/he would only change, life would be perfect. It doesn't work. To be happy, you have to use your inner power. Remember, as much as this frustrates you, no one can give you happiness. Change how you use your power in relationships, release expectations of others and your life will change. Be aware of your presumptions. Are you happy when someone has promises for you to fulfill? Sooner or later someone will always be disappointed. Drop assumptions, drop your disappointments, do your own work, and find your freedom.

Possibly you blame your unhappiness on lack of money or material possessions. Society's objectives, money, fame, and success are wonderful distractions for a time. Certainly it's more fun to have it all, but outside acquisitions do not equate to lasting happiness. Nor are assets ever truly yours. You may lose them at any time, and you can't take them with you when you leave this world. You can only take the love and devotion you give to yourself and others. The love that remains part of your soul and your spirit can never be taken from you. This was one of my lessons when I was diagnosed with cancer. It became immediately apparent that I had been striving for the unimportant all my life.

A Course in Miracles teaches the external world is impermanent and a brief illusion. And in truth, everything in the external world is temporary. You can lose your house, children, spouse, parents, job, car, and any other *possessions*, but self-love, self-acceptance, love for others, forgiveness, and freedom will always remain with your soul. It is who you are that defines you, not your education or your material possessions.

Your life's purpose is to *honor* yourself, create and promote joy, peace, love, and acceptance for *yourself*, and then you automatically give it to others. Before you can experience your purpose, use the knowledge of your inner children to stop placing blame on the external world and accept the fact that you possess the power to choose and create your life.

Thich Nhat Hahn, author of *The Art of Mindful Living* says, *"My actions are my only true belongings. I cannot escape the consequences of my actions. My actions are the ground on which I stand. This requires courage."*

Step Nine

Healing Your Relationships

Myth: When you blame or judge and hold onto resentment, you're punishing and hurting others.

Truth: You only hurt yourself if you carry resentment or cling to negative emotions about another person.

> *Being tolerant does not mean that I share another one's belief. But it does mean that I acknowledge another one's right to believe and obey his own conscience.*
>
> Viktor Frankl

⌘ Activity IX: Find a relationship in your life that needs healing and write about it in your journal. Identify and write about how you want to change the relationship.

Step 9: Most of us have relationships that could be improved. When you heal a significant relationship, you relieve your body of major stress, anxiety, anger, and resentment and open yourself to healing.

Relationships offer your greatest challenges, and significant others are your best teachers. That includes home as well as work. We bring unhealed wounds, unmet needs, and expectations into every relationship expecting another to make us happy. When someone tells me that they have found their true love or soul mate and that he or she "makes me so happy," I know there is a rough road ahead for all the people involved. A soul mate inevitably will bring challenges into your life because they are not perfect. They are human too, as are you. Remember, this book is about forgiveness for being human. We are not ever going to be perfect.

Judgment, again, is the key culprit and the foundation for destruction. It destroys relationships, causes wars and creates almost all other conflicts. When we judge others, we usually criticize them by telling them what *they* are doing wrong. Feeling judged and attacked, the other feels a need to defend, so then defends by striking back, creating a vicious cycle. Once again, attack, defend, attack, and defend! I have several suggestions that may help you be more effective when you are feeling attacked. The following offerings are intended to help and are not meant as criticism. When practiced, these suggestions have the power to change your life though they are typically the opposite of how most people react when under fire:

1. Stop focusing on the other person's behavior. It's a waste of your time.

2. Stop projecting blame on to the other person. It's a waste of your time.
3. Your feelings are all about you and your perceptions, so stop trying to make someone else wrong. It, too, is a waste of your time.
4. Stop thinking about the "wrong" you felt was done to you and bring your focus back to you. Then decide to ask for help to see the situation differently.
5. Then listen to the other person for any truth in their feelings or beliefs. Take responsibility for all that you might have said or done that was thoughtless or hurtful or accusing. There just could be some truth for you to see or hear. Just stop talking and listen carefully to the other person. Hear and learn.
6. Respond with "I will take your opinion under consideration" and then deal with the problem when your defensiveness is gone. After that, you can more rationally compare another's opinion or criticism to your own behavior. Don't respond immediately. Give yourself time to be objective and choose your response if you still believe the situation deserves a response. Very often, after a short time, it doesn't feel as important to respond. You can let it go after you complete #7.
7. Look within, go to your chart and identify specific feelings, and discover why you feel attacked. Remember, your feelings and reactions are all about you.
8. Recognize when you are criticizing another, it speaks volumes about you, the person making the judgment. It says nothing about the one being judged.
9. Your last remaining freedom is your choice.
10. Relinquishing any attachment to outcome is the key to enlightenment.
11. All forgiveness leads to self-healing.
12. Select the people and the experiences you want in your life.

13. Focus only on your abilities and talents and let go of changing the beliefs of others over which you have no control.
14. Take responsibility for your thoughts and your actions, for they create your life situation by situation.
15. Ask God to be with you and help you. Then listen.
16. Look within for the answers.
17. Decide on characteristics you would like to change about yourself, write them in your journal and then set some goals to get the results you desire.

Silence works when being verbally attacked and silence when used correctly feels powerful. In silence, you listen and watch the other person struggling to convince you of your error. My advice is, never defend any criticism directed at you. Instead, listen to hear if there is any truth in the criticism. When you listen, it is easier to respond more positively or calmly. Remove yourself from a situation if someone continues to judge and criticize you.

Find your power! When someone is judging you, listen quietly and say nothing. It works best. An angry person won't hear you anyway. The attacker doesn't know how to respond if you are not defending and he or she is greeted with silence. Defensiveness only prolongs the conversation. Let others have their perceptions and beliefs. You can't change their mind, and they have a right to their beliefs even if they are wrong. It doesn't make them right but *it is* their right. You will learn more by listening and feel powerful by not defending. Just listen and learn. It sounds simple, and it is simple, but it isn't always easy to remember when you are lost in the many emotions of your kids. Be patient with yourself in the lengthy process of knowing and loving yourself. In time you can change the thoughts and actions that don't work for you. I recommend that you review the above suggestions several times and write your feelings on every idea until you get comfortable with what each offers you.

Think of the story about the gift to the Buddha. *After a speech to a crowd of people, a disciple of the Buddha asked him how he could speak to groups, ignore the hecklers, and still be calm and loving to all. The Buddha smiled at his disciple and said, "If someone offers you a gift and you refuse the gift, to whom does the gift belong?"*

The disciple thought and answered with a question, "Does it belong to the one who is attempting to give it to you?"

The Buddha responded, "Yes, people will always try to give you gifts. You don't always have to receive them."

When someone attempts to give you a gift of anger, resentment or blame, just refuse the gift and walk away. It is a very impressive response.

When you are critical of yourself, albeit a habit most of the time, it is impossible to give love and acceptance to others. Be vigilant of your thoughts about yourself and others. Anytime you are judging in any way, you are really judging yourself. Blaming others is just a projection of self-hatred or self-anger. Blame is an expression of disapproval or reproach. Blame denies self-responsibility and implies liability for a crime, or a sin, or at the least an error.

People who are happy with themselves do not judge or blame others. They have no need to criticize or hold others responsible because they are happy within, and they are happy outside as well. When one judges, it doesn't mean that their opinion is true. It means that the person doing the judging is condemnatory. You cannot give to others that which you do not possess. Honor yourself and you contribute love to the world, or remain critical of self and others and create unhappiness within and without. Which do you choose? Happiness is a choice.

We often look for happiness in relationships. We seek to find a "soul-mate." We look for the perfect someone to "*make us happy*" and "*answer all our needs.*" These thoughts are actually a setup for failure, and they imply that you need someone else to fulfill your needs before you can be happy. Society, the entertainment industry, movies, music, commercials all *seem to* supports this disappointing myth. When we think we have found him/her, we feel happy. Everything seems wonderful, but in time, after the glow is tarnished a bit, we begin to see the shortcomings in the other. Again, it is inevitable because no one is perfect.

As the couple become disillusioned, in time the relationship ends and the search to look for the next *right person* begins or we try to change the same person we thought was perfect just a few months ago. Unhappiness is created by attempting to control or change our partner or we feel that he/she is trying to control us. And so the divorce rate continues to rise as more and more people look for another "perfect" partner.

Long-term happiness never comes from outside. Enduring peace and joy are only found inside. There is no perfect partner. With a perfect partner, we would have nothing to learn and no challenge to grow. Unfortunately, we have to experience conflict or pain before we can experience growth and joy, the same way we must see darkness before we can know light. We can only have a continuing relationship with someone else by concentrating on our own ability to stop judging, and accept the complete package.

> Aldous Huxley said in *Time Must Have a Stop* in 1945, "*There is only one corner of the universe you can be certain of improving, and that's your own self.*"

Step Ten

Finding Self-love

Take Time for Yourself

Myth: As we age, we grow wiser.

Fact: As we age, we continue to make the same mistakes until we decide to make different choices and choose to create our life differently.

> *"Things do not change; we change."*
>
> Henry David Thoreau

⌘ Activity X: Allocate quiet time just for you, and study your chart of ICs, especially when you're anxious or troubled about something you have done or said. Forgive your self because you are not perfect or for losing your temper. Ask your self

"Who am I and who do I want to be?" Learn to consciously choose your feelings, your actions and your aspirations.

Step 10*:* Self-love. How do we find self-love? Fear, lack of awareness, disappointment and denial (not being honest with you) are the barriers to wisdom and self-love. To deny is to stay in darkness. To be silent, listen and study your decisions and your actions is knowledge and understanding.

Many believe it is selfish or lazy to reserve special time for your self. It is essential to be selfish sometimes. Solitude challenges you by facing your inner feelings and thoughts. Shopping, movies, TV, sports, romance, etc. are a few of society's distractions which preclude us from looking within and avert us from finding time for contemplation and inner awareness. Distractions are a means to avoid feelings like sadness, loneliness, and fear. Sometimes we need to be side-tracked with fun things and other times when we have deep anger or resentment we need to focus on the reason we are diverting ourselves and work on resolution. Again, if you seek help from a professional counselor, the tasks will be easier and more effective.

Society's values and expectations provide unlimited interesting and exciting external challenges for us to focus on. But looking externally merely delays and obstructs self-growth and prevents you from knowing yourself. Sooner or later you will be forced to look within be it because of incidents such as divorce, illness, failure, death of a loved one or another challenging circumstance. I had every one of these opportunities to change my focus but none motivated me until I was diagnosed with cancer.

My life was a textbook example of my perfected art of

diversion in the form of romance, sports, clothes, cars, jobs, relationships, money, travel, success and other excesses. I was typical. Well, rather than typical, maybe I was more like archetypal of excessive behavior. But I digress. We distract ourselves with romance and all of my other diversions, run from self-love, stuff our feelings, eat too much, drink in excess and focus on work or fun and games, anything outside of ourselves to distract ourselves from feeling or fearing. And sometimes we think we are making ourselves happy and we are temporarily. But sustained happiness is rare and elusive. Today's youth has TV, movies, video games, X Box, sports, in addition to all of the above, none of which encourages contemplation or inner growth.

Today's youth is an angry generation. Suicide rates are climbing in our wealthiest neighborhoods. There are more deaths than ever from car accidents with people under twenty. There is no time for children and teens, in this era, to look within. Just watch the news and look for the negative and fearful. I see it firsthand in my own family. My grandchildren have been rushing to different activities for all of their short lives. They have very little relaxing time to themselves and they are constantly tired. Geshe Kelsang Gyatso says it best below in *Eight Steps to Happiness*, written in 2000,

> *"Everyone wants to be happy and no one wants to suffer, but very few people understand the real cause of happiness or suffering. We tend to look for happiness outside ourselves, thinking that if we had the right house, the right car, the right job, and the right friends we would be truly happy. We spend almost all of our time trying to adjust the external world, making it conform to our*

> *wishes. All our life, we have tried to surround ourselves with people and things that make us feel comfortable secure or stimulated. Yet we have not* found *pure and lasting happiness, even when we succeed.*
>
> In fulfilling our desires, it is not long before our desires change and we want something else. We may find the house of our dreams, but a few months later we feel we need a larger kitchen, an extra bedroom or a larger garden and we begin to think of moving. Or perhaps we meet the "perfect" partner, fall in love and move in together. At the beginning our partner seems to be the most wonderful person in the world, but before long we begin to see faults in him or her. We discover we are no longer in love and soon we are looking for someone else to fulfill our desires. Throughout history human beings have sought to improve their external situation, yet despite all our efforts we are no happier."

Journaling and contemplative time facilitates an understanding of this process and reveals why you feel as you do. Most of us don't like being alone, so we don't give ourselves much alone time. Watching or playing sports, movies, shopping, playing golf, tennis, softball, running, exercising, traveling, socializing, looking for a car or a house or any distraction absolutely does add fun to life and helps you to feel good. None of the above activities are negative, but they *are* diversions from self-knowledge and self-knowledge is the only lasting investment in happiness. When we are always running, we have no time for contemplation and no opportunity to explore exactly what is creating our problems. Consequently, we spend our lives reacting rather than becoming proactive and in being in charge of our own lives. Self-knowledge offers sustained freedom and happiness.

Our society is on the go offering distractions continually for all ages. Teens and the younger generation focus on sports, TV, movies, new video games, newer, stronger, smarter phones, newer fashions, computers, cyberspace, MySpace, boyfriends, and girlfriends. Today the list is endless for all age groups.

I suggest that you consciously set your priorities. Give yourself the gift of time. Time reveals all reasons, feelings, lessons, and opportunities. That's why hindsight is 20/20. Give yourself time to think, and time to discover you. Be proactive rather than reactive. Toys and distractions change, come, and go, but knowledge and insight are the gifts that keep on giving.

Don't be afraid to accept and allow sad or hurt feelings; let them flow and reveal the feelings you choose to release to achieve true freedom. When you can see beneath each emotion and permit the feeling to surface, you can feel it, experience it, and then release the feeling. Liberate your courage to understand, allow, and let go. Shed the tears, or let the sadness and hurt be a part of you and then release them by choice.

Once again, I, at all times, recommend professional counseling to help one cope with the deeper issues that have been burdens for years. It is challenging and complex to do this work all by yourself. Releasing these issues can be painful but it is generally healthy. Seek professional help to lighten the load you carry. If you are on medication or under care of a therapist or doctor, I strongly advise that you make them aware of the internal work you are doing and include them in your effort. Keep them advised of your progress, feelings, and choices.

The purpose of your personal chart is to recognize and accept all parts of you, even if you don't like what you perceive. Just make note of it, and say to yourself, "Wow, I never knew that or never thought about that before," and praise yourself for being aware today. Be honest, accepting, and willing to learn about yourself and how the inner children, born years ago, are still influencing your life today. You'll make changes and find peace. When you're honest with yourself, you can be honest with anyone. As Neale Donald Walsh says in *Conversations with God, Book Three*, "Betrayal of self is the biggest betrayal of all."

Any feeling you uncover and become familiar with is important. Every emotion you reveal requires your love and acceptance. You need no other when you give acceptance to self. When a client admits to jealousy they often follow with, "I hate that part of me." That statement is judgmental and needs to be released. There is a reason for jealousy within you and you need to know the reason. When you hate it and try to shove it aside, it resists. Just recognize and allow and release.

Try to observe your feelings without judgment. Feelings are not negative or positive, they just are. Be Taoist in that respect. When you accept every part and every thought of yours, you have the ability to change. When you are in denial, feelings remain stored in your body. It is possible to change any emotion or feeling, but it's impossible you will reprogram or reverse qualities by denying or berating their existence. Don't chastise and condemn yourself, or you are reinforcing the same harm to you that society is guilty of.

Be kind to those children within you. They need love and acceptance not shame and hatred. You have had enough judgment and criticism from others in your life.

Develop awareness with a commitment to learn, a desire to grow, and a willingness to change direction. Have patience with yourself. Your feelings took years to develop, and you can't change them overnight. I am still working on forgiving myself for not being perfect and probably always will. It seems more difficult to forgive myself than to forgive another, and the easiest conclusion is not to forgive at all since we all seem to expect perfection of everyone and everything. Yet as humans we will never be perfect. Sooner or later we will all fail at something and we will all make mistakes at times. Surely we will do both as long as we are human. That's human. Our response to a perceived *failure* or *mistake* is significant. It's wisest to learn from your experiences and try different actions or responses so that next time there may be an altered outcome. When you want to love yourself, it really does feel better to forgive yourself, learn from your mistakes, and move on. If you learn from any mistake, it is not a failure; it becomes a success in that it taught you about yourself and has given you a different perception to use when a similar occasion arises.

15. *Exercise*: Again, use your journal to write on the following questions.

    Here are some tried and true questions to ask you when you are facing a problem, have an argument or are feeling like a failure:

- How and what can I learn from this mistake? Ask your self if this is an error.
- What was my part in this mistake?
- What is it that I would like to come of this? How can I create a different outcome?
- What is my responsibility now? Who do I choose to be?
- What action do I take if any? (i.e., an apology if indicated or forgiveness if needed)
- If the action is a negative action, ask yourself, "Why do I want to _______?"
- What do I want to come of this situation? What do I want to learn?

Understand and own your motives and stop trying to make anyone else understand. And stop trying to make another wrong. It doesn't feel good for very long.

Statements/affirmations to use:

- I am a kind and loving person.
- I forgive myself for not being perfect. I forgive the other person for not being perfect.
- I will do better next time.
- I love myself and recognize my wonderful qualities.
- I am confident and capable of doing anything I choose.
- I learn from every mistake.

- I love myself and enjoy change and growth.
- I am grateful for the lessons that come my way.

Then release whatever issue that is disturbing you and get on with your life. Let the other person handle the situation their own way. It is their right as long as they are not trying to physically hurt you.

Making mistakes is human. Errors provide opportunities to learn, not to create shame. Every stumble, no matter how insignificant, has a message and a lesson. Just be ready and willing to take responsibility for missteps and your happiness because your choices created your life and you can now create differently.

Being responsible for your own actions changes all dynamics of blame. It prohibits you from accusing others and ends the focusing on what others are "doing to you." When you focus on others, you have no power because you give your it away. While your focus is where it belongs, on you, you preserve your power to make changes. You can then make different choices that enhance your life. Focusing on others drains your life force and wastes your precious time. When you feel hurt, anger, or resentment, you waste your energy, put yourself in a victim role, and feel powerless. Keep your focus on consciously choosing your emotions, beliefs, and roles, and your power and energy remains within you, working for you. Worry always puts you into the future. Stay in the present and you can deal with anything.

Change engenders fear and fear often prevents action. Most people are afraid of change and choose to rationalize a situation rather than risk the outcome. Statistics show that most people will stay with a negative situation rather than make a change that may improve their lives. It is normal for many to fear the unknown, but unfortunately fear keeps you paralyzed. Fear also puts you into the future so remember to stay in the present. The present is always easier to deal with than the illusive future. Recognizing your feelings allows you to see your life differently.

Fear is the driving force under most emotions, but it is often masked by rationalization. For example, "I could make a move now which I would love, but I can't because I don't have the time or the money." Fear thwarts our taking the first and necessary steps to our dreams. If we fear success because of our beliefs that we might fail, we won't try hard enough. If fact we might not try at all in spite of the fact that thousands of self-help books advise you to persist in your dreams and that hard work will reward you with the success you desire. Perseverance and determination generally prevails over fear of any kind. Walt Disney said, "If you can dream you can do it."

Another reason that we are anxious and afraid to make choices, is that we fear we might make a mistake. We are often paralyzed or controlled by fear. We are shy because we worry we might be rejected or laughed at. We avoid intimacy, because if we allow intimacy, they might see who we really are and then reject us. So we reject them first. We are scared to allow our feelings, so we take drugs or drink or spend our pain away. The list of fears is never ending and controls us. Fear creates insecurities and self-doubt in all areas of our lives. Once again, seek the help of a professional counselor for support through the changes.

TV programs, news shows, newspapers, talk shows, magazines, and movies promote and reinforce alarm, concern and anxiety. Local, national and international news are filled with reasons to worry. To name a few, fear of weather, germs, terrorism, death, disease, accidents, and conflict, recession, and inflation. Unfortunately, anxiety, worry, and fear weaken the immune system through the stress they create. My first book, *The Good News; It's Cancer*, is a supportive illustration on how thoughts and anxieties generate disease.

When nauseating fear sets in, I choose to give it to God and quickly reassure myself that I will be okay no matter happens in the future. The Law of Attraction is always at work, and your thoughts create your life. The Law of Attraction, with which many are familiar, says that what you think about is what you attract to you. It is a simple law. Your negative thoughts attract the negative and your positive thoughts attract the positive. Your specific fears could become your reality by your worry or your fears about it. It is similar to the Self-fulfilling prophecy which says that you create the situations in your life by your thoughts. The Abraham-Hicks tapes and books are an excellent source to learn more on the Law of Attraction and manifestation of your dreams.

There are exceptions to every rule (except for death and taxes), and exceptional people have learned to channel universal love and energy through themselves, and back out into the universe. Exceptional people attract the positive to them because they think they can. Worry drains energy; it doesn't energize or motivate. It attracts the negative, keeps you in fear and in the future, thereby inhibiting your actions today.

Worry, guilt and fear also create stress and anxiety in the body, both of which are harmful to your body. Even "good stress" (a promotion, planned move, new baby, engagement, or marriage) takes its toll on your health. Managing stress and anxiety is much easier if you are aware of your feelings, so accept the feelings and transmute them into conscious choices. It is that simple after you have identified your inner children and raised them properly.

When creating your personal chart, you identify many conflicting inner thoughts so don't be confused when you recognize diametrically opposed characteristics within you, i.e., secure/insecure, impatient/patient, stupid/smart, responsible/irresponsible creating self-conflict. Include all conflicting characteristics in your chart. We feel secure about some issues and insecure about others. We feel impatient or patient, intolerant or tolerant depending on the situation and the people involved. It's crucial to recognize that we act, at times, contradictory and polarized. Therein lays the conflict, confusion, and paralysis experienced when you are unable to make a decision.

We can be different people depending on whom we are with. We act and react differently to specific people. Mates are treated differently than your children, although not always. Friends are different depending upon the type of relationship you have with each of them. You will share more with some than with others. To clarify, even when you have made progress in impatience, intolerance, self-criticism, or other traits that you want to change, they should be included in your chart because they still exist within you. They don't ever disappear even if you are aware. They will continue to challenge you. Your awareness helps you to control and reassure them in the future. Add any characteristic that has ever been present in you. Include the "good" inner children such as loving, caring, responsible, giving, intelligent, etc. You are the sum of all your parts: the ones you like and the ones you would rather deny.

16. *Exercise*: Answer the following questions in your journal as honestly as you can:

    - Who are you? What do you think? What do you feel? Try to describe who you think you are as specifically as you can without judgment. Don't limit yourself.
    - Do you ever feel irrational, or that you overreact or feel you weren't yourself today?
    - Identify the feelings you felt before the irrational feelings came.
    - Are you judgmental or critical of yourself? How does it feel to be judged?
    - Do you use many should or shouldn't? These are words that indicate you feel guilty.
    - Do you ever feel out of control? What decisions of yours or events took you there?
    - Do you ever make a choice that you know is going to hurt you later?
    - How often do you feel peaceful and joyful?
    - Do you ever "bite your nose off to spite your face"?
    - Do you worry? Worry keeps you in the future.
    - Do you feel guilty? Guilt is useless and keeps you in the past.
    - Do you ever feel invisible?
    - Are you afraid to be assertive or ask questions in groups?
    - Do you have to be perfect? If so, why? Is perfection expected for others or yourself?
    - Have you forgiven yourself if you don't always meet your or others' expectations?

Don't "should" on yourself! Forgive and forget.

Guilt and worry are destructive and are the two most useless feelings in the universe, yet we live by them. Why? Habit! This does not mean you shouldn't be responsible, but you can be responsible without worry or guilt if you remain in the present.

Study your answers and identify behaviors that aren't working for you and list which behaviors or traits you would like to change. Be specific in your answers. Look for precise areas to work on, such as worry, anxiety, guilt, forgiveness or judgment. Then watch for those areas to reveal themselves in your relationship with others. Take time to ponder on your life and thoughts and always look within for answers.

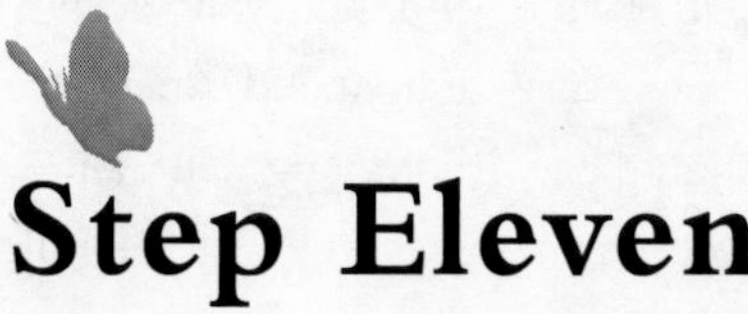

Step Eleven

Embrace Your Purpose, Take Charge

Myth: Your purpose for being is to help others.

Truth: Your purpose for being is to learn self love first and then help others from a healthier, more loving perspective.

⌘ *Activity XI*: Discovering what you believe is the purpose for your life.

Step II: This step helps you discover your destiny. Do you know what your purpose is? As we discussed earlier, the answer is within you, and no other person is your reason for living. Take charge with authority and embrace your purpose. You can choose to make someone else your focus, but you came here to be you, to learn your lessons, and you alone are responsible to discover your purpose. It's impossible to see your true purpose until you have accepted and love every part of you. Then can you hear your Higher Self who will lead you to your objective. Life is a self-evolving circle. You are here to know and love yourself unconditionally and in doing so you will find your way back to God.

Learning about yourself requires a non-defensive, accepting, honest, non-blaming look within to discover who you are. You are the sum of your inner children, your accomplishments, your failures, your every thought and experience. Your observation of self should be without judgment, allowing yourself to accept all of your feelings, the shame, guilt, jealousy, anger, hatred, sadness as well as the happy, funny, strong, smart, etc. They're all the same when you're developing awareness and acceptance. Nothing is negative or positive, as the Taoist says, "It just is." When you know yourself, it is easier to hear your inner wisdom.

When you accept yourself, the second step to self-love is automatic. Honor your needs. Seems simple but is difficult because it's contrary to what you're taught from the moment you're born. Children are called "selfish" by others, and the implication is that people won't like you when you're selfish. You were controlled and manipulated many ways but being called selfish frequently got the wanted results from parents or siblings. Usually, it is unconscious parents, siblings, or teachers doing the manipulating. That said I believe the most important purpose for your life is *to learn how to honor your own needs, accept yourself unconditionally, and fulfill those needs for yourself and then give the same honor and unconditional acceptance to others.*

Few have the ability or purpose to give unconditionally as Jesus did. Mother Teresa was one of a small number in this world although there are many more that we may never know about. But most of us need to learn how to love our own needy, hurting inner children unconditionally before we can take care of ourselves responsibly. We need to raise our ICs with unconditional love, respect, and validation. Doing so will make you better parents to your Inner children as well as your biological children in this world of criticism and expectations and perhaps create more people who can give unconditionally.

17. *Exercise* : Journal on the following question.

    How can you honor yourself? Recognize the actions you would need to take and describe how that would look.

Here are some goals to help you achieve self-honor and self-love:

- Make your first responsibility to yourself. How does that feel?
- Say no instead of yes without guilt if you don't want to do something. How does that feel?
- Say no instead of yes, without guilt, if you don't want to do something. How does that feel? (Repeated because it is the most important to accomplish.)
- Stop criticizing yourself. Can you hear yourself and stop?
- Give yourself a break often. Be complimentary to yourself.
- Lighten up, laugh at yourself. We are funny beings if we can laugh at ourselves.
- Stop expecting perfection; you're not perfect, and you will never be as long as you are human.
- Remember to learn from mistakes. Post-Its were a mistake.
- Take care of your own needs because no one else can as consistently as you can.
- Make time for yourself several times a week.
- Be selfish at times. Try it; it's fun! I love it, enjoy it, and you deserve it too.
- Stop trying to please everyone. (That's not fun!)
- Make positive statements such as, I am strong, beautiful, handsome, accomplished, smart, nice,

successful. (You don't have to believe it; you just have to start saying them.)

- Stop taking others personally. Recognize their actions and words come from their inner children and only defines them not you. Your actions and words define you.
- And as my good friend Carolyn tells me, "Build a bridge and get over it!"

Unconditional self-acceptance and love is the biggest challenge we face. If you are able to accomplish that goal you will find joy and peace. In Neale Donald Walsch's book *Conversations with God, Book* 3, the God of his understanding, says the following:

> *"Betrayal of yourself in order not to betray another is betrayal nonetheless. It is the highest betrayal."* In the book, God also says, *"Do you really think that if you force another to keep a promise that you will have escaped injury? I tell you this: More damage has been done to others by persons leading lives of quiet desperation (that is doing what they felt they 'had' to do) than ever was done by persons freely doing what they wanted to do.*
>
> *"When you give a person freedom you remove the danger, you don't increase it.*
>
> *"Yes, letting someone 'off the hook' on a promise or commitment made to you may look like it will hurt you in the short run, but it will never damage you in the long run, because when you give the other person their freedom, you give yourself freedom as well. And so now you are free of the agonies and the sorrows, the attacks on your dignity and your self worth that inevitably follow*

> *when you force another person to keep a promise to you that he or she does not want to keep.*
>
> *"The longer damage will far outweigh the shorter—as nearly everyone who has tried to hold another person to their word has discovered."*

In my humble opinion, Chapters 12 and 13 in *Conversations with God, Book* 3 have presented the most accurate and ideal description of a desirable relationship. They offer love and freedom and trust, all lovely components of God's love. I believe it is an inspirational passage that describes how God feels about honoring one another, and it reveals how expectations of others create judgment and problems for us. It's the exact opposite of the expectations that society imposes.

> *"He who wishes to secure the good of others has already secured his own."*
>
> Confucius

Confucius says that once you have secured unconditional love and acceptance for yourself then can you give it to others. Does everyone have the same reasons for being here? Are the reasons universal? I believe the answer is yes. However, not everyone will accomplish their goals at the same time. We have free will, so we get to choose when we want to learn and grow, and it is *our right* to decide our own time frame. It is *our right* to make personal choices. People are ready at different times for individual reasons. Only you can decide that for yourself. You can learn it now or learn it later. The universe will continue to present opportunities until you recognize the lessons needed for your purpose.

What is our second purpose in life?

To give that same unconditional love you have found for yourself to all others. After you possess self-love, you can give freely to others without resentment. You no longer try to manipulate, guilt, judge, or criticize others because you no longer allow yourself to be manipulated, guilty, or judged. You no longer feel a need to control others because you are in control of yourself. And you will not allow anyone else to control you. You are on your way to freedom and by your example and by your actions you will help others.

"Our life is what our thoughts make it."
Marcus Aurelius Meditations, second century AD

Why is it important to know the answers to these questions?

Knowing and loving yourself makes it possible for you to live a purpose-driven life. Possessing that wisdom reduces your desire to seek more of the distractions in the world. It decreases your need for external approval and fulfillment. You can enjoy all that the world offers without dependence because you are complete, with your Inner Wisdom available to you at all times. Your relationship with your Creator is clear and no longer obstructed. You have released the true happiness buried deeply inside you as you do this internal work. The higher you emerges as you honor and love yourself and when you do, you are able to automatically give honor and love to others without resentment

Many family stories are similar to mine. My mother was one of six children, as was my father. Mom was born in the middle of six children and dad was the youngest of six. Both sets of grandparents were Catholic, started a family early, and were overwhelmed with the huge families they created. They worked hard, grew their own food, were poor, struggled to survive, and were unable to meet their children's many emotional needs. My grandparents and parents suffered through the Depression, worked hard to get through each day, and none of their children received the love or attention each needed. Instead, they were forced to leave school at twelve years old to work and contribute to the family in every way they were needed. Unfortunately, this life did not prepare my parents for proper parenting. My parents did the best they could and I loved them and don't blame them, but it did create problems for me. On the positive side, those problems also contributed to my internal strength.

One parent (my father, the youngest and only boy of six children) was in many ways spoiled by his older sisters and received very little discipline. He was frequently left on his own, developed a raging temper, and everyone was afraid of him so he had no teaching or discipline. He was angry, sometimes violent, loving at times, critical at others. He was controlling and had great expectations of his first child, me.

My mother was a middle child of six girls so she was lost in the crowd and never received much attention or affection. She felt ordinary, sometimes invisible, and had low self-esteem. She thought she was ugly and plain, so when my handsome father showed interest in her, she felt honored. They married without any preparation for his anger or for marriage. She, unable to assert herself, silently watched my father's rage, was afraid of him, and retreated into herself. She rarely shared her feelings and was silent through my dad's outbursts. She did not have any confidence in herself to change anything. He never hit her, but he did hit me, many times.

I was the oldest child of two and the one of the many second generation in a large Italian family. My brother, seven years younger than I, as a boy, had more freedom than I for two reasons: because he was a boy and because my parents relaxed their restrictions with child number two. I resented both deeply. I felt he was the favorite, which hurt me and made me very angry with all of them. In reality, I was the favored child (I discovered much later), but that was not my truth from my childhood perspective. My brother was sickly and received continual attention from my mother. I felt abandoned. Mother rarely had time for me because she worked hard and also had a sick child. I was healthy and left to fend for myself. When I came home from school with my report card showing all A's and one B, my dad would just point to the B and say, "What's that B doing there?" He never praised me for the A's. He did spank me in his rage at other times and my mother was so afraid of him that she did not stop him. As he dragged me off to my room, she would say, "Don't hit her on the head." I would just look at her and wonder why she didn't stop him. I was too young to know she was afraid. At seven or eight, I felt angry and abandoned by her.

I, too, was afraid of my father and was not allowed to show any feelings or anger. Whenever I cried, I was told to stop crying or I would get more to cry about. By the time I was ten, I was a raging, angry, and repressed child with no outlet to feel or show my anger. By the time I was thirty with unresolved anger about the repression and control in my childhood, I was beginning to show the anger externally, and was called a bitch by many.

I seemed to lose my temper easily. I was hurt and took every negative comment personally. I was also labeled as unreasonable, over-reactive, too sensitive and other equally destructive names, and I was beginning to believe them even though I was always hurting. This fed into my feeling that there was something terribly wrong with me, though I knew not what. I just knew that I didn't feel good enough but I didn't know why. It was very confusing to me because I was always trying to please others and yet I still seemed to be failing even at people pleasing.

After counseling others for years and developing cancer, I finally found my way to happiness and health and this process is the result of all of my work. I personally possessed almost all of the ICs on the Comprehensive List of Universal Children. With my help, all of my clients also identified the same inner children that I did. And those that worked the process seriously have also found what I have today—self-love, peace and happiness.

In fact my experience is common and remarkable only in the fact that so many of us feel the same way about ourselves. Your issues might be different but the feelings, created by events in my childhood, seem to be fairly universal in my coaching and counseling experience. After reading my book, *The Good News: It's Cancer*, men and women alike wrote to tell me that they identified with my feelings and as they read, they felt I was writing their story. But I, the child, felt alone, different, abandoned, not good enough, unlovable, anxious, afraid, angry, victimized, guilty, not respected, not validated, and all of the others in the Universal Chart. I feel very blessed to have learned all that I know today and I know if I can do it, so can you.

18. *Exercise*: The objective of these questions is to gain more insight into your parents and your childhood. Ask yourself the following questions, and document the answers in your journal:

    - How old were your parents when they got married? Most were too young to know how to be parents.
    - How old were they when their first child was born? Young parents probably were overwhelmed and ill-prepared for a baby leaving both the baby and the parents frustrated with many unanswered needs.
    - How old were they when you were born? Children born close together are challenging in some ways, and the parents hopelessly struggle by having two children so close in age. Think about what those problems might have been. Think about whether you were able to get attention or your needs met by parents who were overwhelmed and ill prepared, raising multiple children, and untrained for parenthood.
    - Where were you in the birth order? Are you the first, youngest, middle, or in between several children in your family? Birth order often builds common attributes. It would be helpful to read a book on the effects of birth order on children.
    - If you had older siblings, how did they treat you when you were a young child? Were they mean or nice to you? If so, what did that feel like? If you can't remember, imagine what a three-year-old might feel if s/he had an older brother or sister that was mean to him/her. At seven, I was nasty to my brother just because he was born and took all the attention away from me. This is common, unfortunately. Were you

the older brother or sister that was angry when a new baby came along (like I was) and took all of your mom's attention away from you? All these feelings are very normal in children and create feelings of being ignored, not good enough, jealousy, anger, disappointment, resentment, and others. Add any you can identify to your chart.

- How did they treat you, as you grew older into your teens? How angry were they? How angry were you?
- How do you relate to these same siblings today? Do you try to please them? Do they try to control you or tell you what to do? Do you "walk on eggshells" when around them? How are your family get-togethers? Do you revert back to childish feelings around them? Note these feelings or behaviors, and write them in any of your circles. The order is not important. Every circle on your chart is vital. Star any circle that you recognize as used frequently.
- What names did they call you and what did they say about you? How did they describe you? For example: pest, stupid, fat, ugly, cute. Whatever was said to you or about you add to circles on your chart. As I noted earlier, I added "bitch" to my chart because I was called that by some.
- Did your parents treat any of you differently? Did they show favoritism? Did they treat boys and girls differently? If so how did that feel to you? Were you the favorite or second best or even feel third best? Add any new emotions, roles, or beliefs to your chart.
- Were they strict or lenient with you? How did you feel about either?

- Were they critical of you or ever tell you that they were disappointed in you? If so, this can create shame in a child. Were you confused? Are you critical of yourself?
- Do you ever feel guilt and/or anger around your parents or siblings? If so, why?
- Did your parents show affection and tell you that they loved you?

Write your answers to significant questions in your journal. When finished, read your answers and identify all feelings, roles, and beliefs and add them to your chart. Reading through your answers will also give you more insight about your childhood. If you can't remember how you felt, just imagine how a child your age might have felt in the same situation.

Consider what your mother and father might have been experiencing. Imagine also about what your siblings might have felt at the same time. Can you relate any of that to how your family interrelates today at gatherings? Is there competition amongst any of you? Add any thoughts to your journal about your present relationships with family members. If you identify any other feelings, add them to your circles.

You may wonder how these exercises, related to your childhood, affect your purpose in life. Negative beliefs and feelings from childhood prevent you from filling your purpose to love yourself unconditionally in your adulthood. These negative (and some positive) roles, beliefs or feelings stay with you for life, until you find resolution within yourself. By clearing out these feelings, forgiving, and moving on, you can truly love yourself unconditionally. Making peace with the past is a mandatory aspect of learning self-love.

An Irish Blessing

Always remember to forget
The things that made you sad.
But never forget to remember
The things that made you glad

Step Twelve

Hear Your Inner Wisdom

Ask for Gentle Lessons

Myth: It is bad luck or poor planning when grave things happen to us.

Truth: Everything that "happens to us" is an opportunity to grow and discover a better way of living, thinking and being.

> *"When we are no longer able to change a situation we are challenged to change ourselves."*
>
> Viktor Frankl

⌘ *Activity XII*: The goal of this activity is to develop the sense of hearing your inner wisdom. Reflect on past serious or depressing events that occurred in your life and write about them in your journal. Recall any lessons you identified or learned from each event. Put your thoughts in your journal. Did you hear the voice within guiding you and giving you answers? It's there. You just have to listen for it and pay attention to the questions you are asked or the answers you receive. Sometimes it is just a thought that passes through your mind.

Step Twelve is to guide you through the process of trusting it is your intuition you are hearing. Once you've identified the voices of your ICs and have learned how to love them, satisfy their fears, and quiet them, you become more proficient at differentiating the voices of the inner children and the voice of your inner wisdom. Your inner wisdom without fail brings peace to you. That's how you distinguish the difference between wishful thinking and inner wisdom. Wishful thinking is not always peaceful because it is usually something you covet, so there are desires attached. Your inner wisdom simply speaks the truth. Your inner wisdom is peaceful and reflects simplicity and love. The awareness and acceptance you cultivate in this process allows you to see situations and people differently, especially if you ask for God's help. Most of us forget to ask God for help. We usually tell God what we want, but we don't allow Him to deliver the goods in His way.

When you accept and recognize every event in life as an opportunity to learn, you gain from every experience, especially the harsh or severe ones. When an incident that you perceive as enjoyable or victorious occurs, who do you become? How do you conduct yourself when you win? How do you behave when you lose? Reflect and journal on these questions. Remember to observe your behavior without judgment during the process.

Then reflect on an incident in the last week that irritated

or angered you and consult your personal chart. Identify any active feelings, as many as you can, and list them in your journal. Some of the questions are intentionally repetitive. In changing years of deep rooted programming, it takes practice before you are able to consistently change long standing reactions. This process takes time and work, but it is successful if you want to change and continue to practice. Just a reminder, you are capable of achieving miracles. As Nike says in their commercials, "Just do it!".

19. *Exercise*: Questions to contemplate on and write about in your journal:

    - What makes you feel good? Why?
    - When do you become generous, friendlier, more outgoing? Why is that?
    - When do you feel good about yourself? Which choices make you feel better?
    - Are you jealous if something good happens to someone around you? Does it matter who it is?
    - When you do well, do you share the credit with others or do you take all the glory?
    - Do you feel you deserve to do well or are you afraid it will be taken from you?
    - Do you resent lack of recognition or credit?
    - Do you think you deserve recognition or credit?
    - Do you need recognition or credit? Why?
    - Are you surprised by any of your answers? If so, what surprises you?
    - How would you describe yourself if someone did not know anything about you?

Again, take as much time as you need to reflect on these questions before you answer them. Refer back to your chart, and list the IC's driving your behavior. Notice the level of your insecurity or the low/high self-esteem within. Every discovery is a plus. The more of yourself you acknowledge and allow, the more aware you become. When one characteristic doesn't work for you, decide to change to one that does. Empower yourself and choose to be proactive rather than reactive.

Self-observation without judgment is amazing and powerful. It removes frustration, identifies the problem, and allows you to change your reactions and actions. Observing yourself in the good times is easy. Viewing yourself in a negative situation is much more difficult. We are human and will make mistakes, feel anger and overreact. It is not that you will ever be perfect on this earth. What really matters is how you react when you do make a mistake, are in the wrong, or say something hurtful in anger. Quickly accept that you are not perfect, forgive yourself and then make amends, apologize or forgive another. If you can accomplish this you indeed have made wonderful progress. You have begun the living with self-love and are improving your life daily and surely.

When someone hurts your feelings or you get angry, you are taking their behavior personally and are responding from the hurt that you choose to feel. You are allowing someone outside of yourself to hurt you. Choose differently because hurt frequently and quickly converts into anger. It is easy to take hurtful comments personally, but words and emotions and beliefs that come from another person are not about you. It reveals the nature of the one person voicing the beliefs, etc. It also reveals their inner children.

As mentioned earlier, we don't recognize the softer feelings preceding anger or irritation, (i.e., defensiveness, not respected, not validated, "not good enough," misunderstood, and unloved). The softer feelings come and go so quickly and the strongest reaction that you feel, anger, remains in you and continues to disturb your peace. Anger, the most frequently recognized emotion, forms early in life. A child cries, and if he/she doesn't receive the desired attention, the child cries louder and harder. You have been conditioned from childhood to use anger, completely unaware of other feelings inside. In a disagreement, you recognize you dislike what was said and you are already conditioned to feel anger. Anger is the emotion you learn to use early on and you are also conditioned by your parents' reaction to your anger. If your parents were permissive, then you were allowed to show and express the anger. If your parents (or one parent) did not allow anger or punished you for expressing it, then you learned to fear and stuff your anger and feared expressing it. Or you rebelled and punished your parents. Neither method is healthy without identifying the feelings underneath the anger. Anger is a warning. It tells you that many of your needs are being neglected either by you or others.

20. *Exercise*: Answer the following questions in your journal as honestly as possible because they will reveal additional information about your beliefs and emotions. Find other inner children that need to be added to your chart and enter them in the circles of your chart.

By this time you might need to pencil in more circles on your chart.

This picture says it all.

- Do you feel sad, hurt, hopeless, angry, irritated, victimized? Identify as many feelings as possible. Identify which IC is creating these feelings and identify behaviors by others that cause you to feel the above emotions.
- Do you blame others or do you take responsibility for your actions? (victim or responsible)
- Do you focus on the other persons' behavior or are you focusing on your own behavior? Remember the only change you can make is within you.
- Do you look for solutions or do you focus on the problem? (negative or positive)
- Do you criticize yourself, or do you accept that you may not be perfect and that everyone makes mistakes? (perfectionist or critic)
- Do you feel you can learn from mistakes or are you afraid of making mistakes? (afraid or open to learning)

- Do you expect perfection of others? (same)
- How do you feel if you break a promise to someone? (i.e., guilty, super responsible, controlled,)
- Identify your feelings if someone breaks a promise to you. (Betrayed, allowing, accepting or controlling, rigid, and critical). If so, your lesson is to release the person from the promise and fulfill your own needs.
- Could you have done anything differently to change the outcome? (open, flexible)
- Do you beat yourself up mentally? (critical and judgmental)

"All honor's wounds are self-inflicted."

Andrew Carnegie

Life is educational and we must strive for objectivity so we can release judgment. When you judge your behaviors then you are the judge, not the observer and you lose objectivity. It's about choice, accepting oneself, developing self-awareness and reprogramming the old toxic beliefs of the five-year-old or the eighteen-year-old inside. My dad used to tell me he went to the school of "hard knocks." The "hard knocks" come along when we are not listening to our inner wisdom and are ignoring what we need to learn. Each "hard knock" is an opportunity to learn. Don't lose the lesson.

When feeling sad or out of peace and joy try looking inward to find the active ICs. Focus inwardly on your feelings. Examine the situation, identify your contribution to the problem and determine what your lessons are. Ask, "How can I learn from this?" How can I see this differently? What actions make me feel best? Are you the teacher or the learner or both? Your future peace of mind will be a major contributor to your ability to learn and grow in your relationships.

Choose to believe there are lessons to learn in every event and obstacle in your life. There are no accidents, just opportunities. This will help you to recognize the lessons as they occur rather than just reacting to the events. When you are in touch with your feelings, you'll find it easier to recognize the opportunity. If you are not in peace and joy, then you are being offered an opportunity to learn. Any feeling is important and should be identified as soon as possible. See Universal List. Failure or disappointment is an opportunity. Arguments, disagreements, and misunderstandings are opportunities; a daily lesson and reminder is road rage. Don't let others provoke you into a fight. Walk away (or drive away).

The following examples are especially accommodating and supportive of the advice offered in this book.

Example One: If you are with a group of friends and one person seems especially critical of you and continues to direct hurtful or embarrassing comments to you, what would be a spiritually appropriate reaction? Above all else, you should never remain in a situation that is physically or verbally abusive to you. Self-love requires self-protection and physically removing yourself when necessary would be appropriate. If it is not problematic for you and if you stay in the group, remember that what another says about you does not define you, their words and actions define them. If you don't join the attacker in his/her negativity by defending and then attacking back, you don't give any energy or credibility to the situation. Rather than attack the other in return for his hurtful comments, it is much wiser and more powerful to smile, remain silent, or excuse your self for a time.

Walk away with dignity and do not let yourself be the one that perpetuated or agreed to hurt someone else. Refuse to join with someone out of control. Recognize that hurt people hurt people. Forgive them and walk away.

Example Two: If you are afraid of a situation, person or illness then you are not using your complete mind powerfully to work for you. You are actually choosing to feel weak and victimized and when you make the choice to be in fear, you lose your power completely. If you stay in the present rather than the future, you can choose to believe that you have the ability to handle anything that is put in your path. If you are in fear, you are in the future. If you are in guilt, you are in the past. The safest place to remain in is the present because the present time is all that we have. Worrying about the past or present is a waste of your time. Stay in the present, take your power back and release any fear, worry, judgment or guilt to God, repeatedly if it returns.

> *"Love is the only force capable of transforming an enemy to a friend."*
>
> Martin Luther King

Love is indeed a powerful force. When you love and honor yourself, life is amazing. Some say it is easier to be happy with money and that's true to a point, but money itself will never bring the kind of peace and freedom to which we are entitled. I once believed that money would buy me freedom, but once I reached my financial goals, I discovered I still wasn't free! I had all I ever wanted materially, but I was still encumbered by the emotional baggage I carried in my mind. The critical and judgmental children within were my problem and created most of my problems as they are causing yours. Childhood conditioning never evaporates until we find our true self and reframe our beliefs and thoughts.

You have a little you sitting on your shoulder, following you around every day, telling you constantly that you are not good enough, not smart enough, not pretty or handsome enough, not successful enough, not thin enough, not rich enough, giving you these and many other negative messages. I often say to my clients, "If you talked to me the way you talk to yourself, I wouldn't feel very good either." Walter Crawford Kelly expressed it this way: *"We have met the enemy and the enemy is us."*

> *"Why do you see the speck in your neighbor's eye but do not notice the log in your own eye? First take the log out of your own eye and then you will see clearly to take the speck out of your neighbor's eye."*
>
> Luke 6:41–42

I love this parable. It sends a droll, intriguing and memorable message. It is a reminder that your focus needs to be on your own behavior. Although I find the phrasing of the parable droll and witty, its message clearly illustrates a humorless and significant problem within all of us. It is what we all do every day until we learn a better way. We are so busy judging other people that we never take the time to recognize our own judgment. When you focus on someone else's' behavior you are making the choice to block your Inner Wisdom.

Your happiness really does depend on how well you know yourself and why you make your choices. You can choose to be happy, or you can choose to be right. Choosing to be right does not always make you happy for long. It takes great effort to continue to prevail in unimportant issues considering all the different perceptions of the millions out there. And why is it so important to be right in another persons' opinion? Why not focus that energy on yourself and your own self-awareness? Then you can really reap the rewards of being right about yourself. Choose not to focus on another's action rather focus on your own behavior and happiness. Then you are proactively choosing and not reacting. *That's what truly puts you in charge of your life.*

What are your obstacles to peace? In the exercises, we have discussed and identified hundreds of barriers to your peace. What are your specific IC challenges and barriers to hearing your Inner Wisdom? Fortunately you now know you have many to choose from! They will continue to greet you and test you daily. But now you are prepared! You have your personal IC chart which gives you all the information you need at a glance. Now that you know which feelings are taking your peace away, you can reverse any negativity to positive with self-love. Give the time, respect and the love to yourself that you deserve and that you have been waiting for. Pay attention to those IC's, love them, reassure them and it is a major achievement and a triumphant achievement for you. You are a winner!

Don't waste your time with outside distractions. Remember your purpose, turn around and walk away. Using this process allows you to see the rage and anger existing in everyone of all ages. Rampant road rage is the best example, and is so easy to identify. Drivers are often angry, in a hurry or very slow; they are competitive, hostile, rude, combative, and use vulgar finger gestures on the road to complete strangers. And often they evoke the same reaction in us, and we respond the same way.

On the road, I see blatant and senseless out of control behavior in otherwise very nice people, and I used to be a frequent participant of this group. The unhappiness, rage, anger, hurt, victimization, misunderstandings, and disagreements are also very conspicuous in our personal and professional lives. There is jealousy toward and from co-workers and families; competitiveness, a feeling that there is not enough to go around; and I have to get there first. Ghandi said we must become the change we want to see in this world. If you see every event in your life as an opportunity to learn about another aspect of yourself, you are utilizing life, as you should: an opportunity to grow wiser and happier. Francis Bacon, in 1625 Essays, said, *"A wise man will make more opportunities than he finds."*

Challenges and opportunities appear in *all* relationships because it's inevitable that sooner or later one of the two people involved will respond contrary to the other's belief. Any problem that takes away your peace and joy is an obstacle to your peace, a challenge and an opportunity to learn. Lessons come in all sizes, shapes, and scenarios. The only method to hear your inner voice/wisdom and feel peace and joy consistently is to take the inevitable time to get to know you and love that self without conditions.

It takes brutal honesty, self-awareness, self-acceptance, learning, and growth to see life differently, change toxic self-talk and learn how to honor yourself and others. Self- love is rarely accomplished because it is so challenging. We make our life problematical; God doesn't. We make decisions; God doesn't. We choose our actions; God doesn't. Your life is created by your choices. We were given free will to make choices. And many of our choices and judgments hurt us simply because we don't know how to choose any differently so our IC's choose for us. A prerequisite for change is seeing and thinking differently before you are able to choose a better path for yourself. The good news is, through this process you can choose to see any situation/problem/irritation differently. It will transform your life and in time reveal your life's purpose. The process of change happens one day at a time, and it starts today. Benjamin Franklin said, "*The world is full of fools and faint of hearts; and yet everyone has courage enough to bear the misfortunes, and wisdom enough to manage the affairs of his neighbor.*"

Step Thirteen

Learning Forgiveness

Give Yourself a Break!

"It is by forgiving that one is forgiven."

Mother Teresa

⌘ Activity XIII: Unconditional forgiveness of self and others.

Step Thirteen is the step to forgiveness. It is time to give your self a break and rebuild the broken places. Forgiveness is commonly perceived as a sacrifice you perform for someone else. You "let the other person off the hook" or "forgive and forget." You do it because it is the "right thing to do." You forgive because you are the "better person." In reality, forgiveness is for you and your benefit, not for the other person. When you forgive, you release the stress within you and liberate your body. This was yet another revelation for me as a result of cancer! Self-forgiveness is the most crucial forgiveness of all because it releases toxins from your body, making it easier for your body to be healthy.

Holding on to anger, torment, disappointment, hurt, displeasure, or rancor toward another person burdens *your* body and mind, stressing *your* immune system, and causing hormonal distress. It only hurts your cells and your body. Forgiveness relieves you of that burden and enhances healing. When you forgive someone, you don't need to condone the situation, and you never need associate with the person again. You can choose never to see the person again. Your mind is the only important part of forgiveness. Forgive the person in your mind, release your anger or hurt, and you have forgiven. It doesn't matter what you do or don't do with the other person. He or she need never know about your forgiveness. Forgiveness releases you not them. What they choose to feel is their business.

It's never too late to forgive. You can forgive parents, relatives, or friends who have passed on from this life. It is an internal process, so you can have an internal dialogue with one who has passed. Even if you can't hear them speaking to you, though you will if you listen, you can say all that you want and release the emotions involved. Since forgiveness is an inside job, you can say anything you want to the person, in any tone you like, and they can and will hear you. Again the importance is not their hearing you but your letting go of the toxic emotions you've carried over the years. I've facilitated many two-way conversations between my clients and parents who have passed, usually resulting in liberation from past anger and hurts. It helped them find peace and resolution on very old issues. The transformative peace that follows with my clients' forgiveness and with my personal forgiveness is always amazing.

True forgiveness is an internal process which resolves and releases any blame or judgment of yourself or another. You don't need the other person for true forgiveness. If you choose to forgive, you automatically release your hurt and negative feelings. Forgive because it feels better to think they were doing the best they could at the time and it lightens your load. You need never interact again with the other person although sometimes it is helpful to you. You can choose how you forgive. Forgiveness is choosing to release the hurt, anger, resentment, or rancor that you carry for the other person. Forgiveness is in the mind and helps you. It is not an act that you perform for someone else.

More importantly, I urge you to forgive *yourself*. As humans, we are encumbered by self-judgments and criticisms that stress our bodies and minds which are capable of eventually wearing us down, leading to illness. Failing to forgive yourself can place you at risk of unconsciously believing you are not deserving of healing, sending a hidden message to your body and creating an unseen obstacle to your healing. Forgiving yourself is more important to your health than forgiving someone else. You need to forgive yourself for not being perfect in every way. No one is perfect! General George Patton said, "If a man does his best, then what else is there?"

Journal about the mistakes you believe you have made. Writing on painful buried memories and criticism piled within you assists in releasing the toxins attacking your body. Write whenever you find yourself criticizing or judging yourself or others. Write about childhood messages that generated feelings of guilt or anger or hurt within you.

Every time you write about your guilt or anger, finish with the words, "I forgive myself for not being perfect." Then say it out loud: "I forgive myself." You don't have to believe what you are saying at first; just say it. Your body believes what you say, and soon your mind will follow and believe, and you have taken an important step toward health. Every time you feel yourself judging or being impatient or critical of yourself or another, immediately give yourself forgiveness. Literally tell yourself that you forgive yourself for judging or being impatient, whatever the case. Acknowledge that you are human, that you will make mistakes and you love yourself anyway. It gives you a long overdue release from a need for perfection.

My relationship with my daughter is an example of the power inherent in self-forgiveness. This story also exemplifies that self-forgiveness is more significant than being forgiven by another. I was in my fifties before I realized that I needed no forgiveness from anyone except myself since I had always been my worst critic.

The following narrative is from my first book, *The Good News; It's Cancer.*

> *When I had cancer the first time, I knew I had many relationships to rectify and change. The most important one was with my daughter, Susan, then in her early thirties. It was one relationship that I believe contributed most to my development of cancer. She was my only child, and it was no accident that both cancers were in my reproductive organs, the breast, and uterus.*
>
> *I knew now that it was time to face the long-standing*

anger between my daughter and me. The following is an excerpt from my book that describes what was the most powerful interaction in my life that would help me deal with cancer and change my life forever. In retrospect it seems simple, but it was not a simple lesson for me and it has not been simple for the many I have taught or counseled over the years. Forgiving myself for not being perfect was foreign and difficult to accomplish, but it was necessary for a healthy life. It was the first major step towards developing self-love and taking my power back.

The relationship between us is difficult to explain. Susan and I were close and loved each other, but underlying the closeness between us was anger on both of our parts. She never forgave me for leaving her father, and she was still angry because I was not the traditional mother that she wanted. I was frustrated that I could never reach her, but I didn't know how. She was a strong young lady, and I was afraid to approach her because of the guilt I still carried from leaving her father and "ruining" her life. I'd known for years that we needed to talk, but I avoided it and never found the courage. Most of the time over the last four or five years, I deceived myself into believing that because I was a more traditional grandmother, she had shed her anger. I deluded myself because it was easier to accept even though I was aware that she was still angry on a deep level that even she didn't understand. She was in therapy but had never resolved her feelings about her father or me. I was definitely afraid of going there. I didn't know how to deal with it, so I didn't.

Now that I had breast cancer and had become more enlightened by my sessions with Dr. Sylvest, I knew that it was time for us to talk. I was convinced that this was the single most important issue that needed resolution, and I didn't want to carry these destructive feelings any longer. It was time to face my past, deal with the negative and damaging feelings, and move on. I didn't want to die of cancer. I wanted to survive. I wanted to live! I could put it off no longer!

But how? By this time, I had begun to meditate. Through my reading, I was learning the benefits of meditation and knew it was important to health. My family doctor, Dr. Leslie Teets, encouraged meditation and supported the benefits of meditation. I was meditating, and it was working. It calmed me when my anxieties about my health were high. It made it easier to deal with the diagnosis I was living with by creating peace inside of me. I was no longer as terrified. I began meditating on the dilemma of how to approach my daughter. I needed some answers and direction. Still weighing heavily on my mind was the most important of all, telling my daughter about the cancer and talking to her about the past. I was scared as hell of this and didn't want to do it. However, I had no choice.

I had known for years that I needed to talk with Susan, but every time I tried, I would sense her anger and succumb to my fear of her reaction. The few times that I had attempted to talk to her, she would turn away and refuse to talk to me. I began to fortify my courage. She had to know, so I called her husband. Slightly cowardly, I suppose in retrospect, but it was a first step.

I told him that I was flying to Rochester, told him the reason, and asked him to pick me up at the airport. Then I called Susan and told her I was coming for a visit. Dan, her husband, picked me up at the airport, and I conveyed everything that had transpired to date. We decided that Susan and I needed time alone. He was well aware of her anger and feelings about her childhood and me, so he suggested we take a walk that night.

After dinner, I suggested that Susan and I go for a walk. Susan is a stunningly beautiful woman. She is slim, about 5'6" tall, with thick, long, raven black hair that curls wildly in every direction. She has big, beautiful, round, brown eyes that show her soul when she is happy. Tonight, however, her eyes were not showing her soul. Her brow was furrowed, her mouth grim, her eyes tired, and she sounded irritated when she replied that she didn't want to go. She was exhausted and wanted to relax.

Dan spoke up and said, "I think you two should go, and I'll care for the kids."

She looked especially annoyed. Her exact reply was, "What have you two cooked up? Why are you pushing me when I don't want to go?"

I blurted out, "We need to talk!" I didn't know what else to say. Clearly she was annoyed with both of us, but she relented and we went for our walk.

As we walked along in a nearby park, oblivious to the surrounding beauty, I shared my diagnosis and what I had learned from Dr. Sylvest. Dr. Sylvest suggested that the guilt from the divorce, the feelings of inadequacy, the belief of my failure in the roles of motherhood and wife, could be affecting me now and had probably contributed to the development of cancer. It was imperative for both of us to confront our past issues for our future health and happiness. I spoke of my feelings about being her mother. I said I knew she had never forgiven me for leaving her father and creating a lifestyle that she hated, and that I knew I wasn't the perfect mother in her mind. I told her how badly I felt all these years for "failing" her, her father, and my mother. I said I knew she and they had wanted me to be different. As I began to say what I had never verbalized before, I had an incredible flash of insight that it was not important that she forgive me. Truly significant to my recovery was that I needed to forgive her, but most importantly I needed to forgive myself. This was truly a revelation! I always thought I needed her forgiveness. Until that moment, I was not aware that I was the person that needed to do the forgiving. My task was to forgive her for her anger and rejection and forgive myself for not being perfect. I didn't have to be perfect for me or anybody else! I had only to accept myself as I was. I had no consciousness that this desire to be the model wife, mother, and daughter was a killer. It had been eating away at me for all of these years. In my heart and mind, I'd worried for so long that I wasn't perfect and I condemned myself because I wasn't.

I was totally oblivious of my own anger because Susan and others reminded me frequently that I was an inadequate mother. Until this moment, I never realized how angry I was at myself for disappointing everyone. My focus was on her anger with me, so I never considered my own feelings of anger. The guilt I carried since my first marriage concealed the anger I felt toward Susan from the time she was five years old. I was shocked to feel this surface from me. I could still clearly see her little black curly five-year-old head walking away from me and remember how frustrated I felt. Even at that early age, she wouldn't talk to me, and I didn't know how to reach her.

Over the years, her anger rarely allowed me to forget her disappointment in my mother role. I didn't know how to express my love for her because I had never been taught how to love myself. Because I didn't love myself, I was unable to show real love to her or others. As I spoke that night, I was uncovering the anger I felt because she had punished me for twenty-five years. Her anger created my guilt. I had hurt her with the divorce. I tried, many times, to show my love through material gifts, but it never worked for long. It was a short-term reprieve. She responded briefly to the gifts, but it was not the way to her heart. She wanted me to prove I loved her and I didn't know how. There was no blame in all of these revelations, only a wonderful insight to what had happened and how we could "fix" it finally!

After I finished talking, I felt much lighter. It felt wonderful, freeing, and fulfilling. A heavy burden had been lifted with this new insight. I was able to forgive her and, more importantly, forgive me for being imperfect. I no longer felt a failure. I felt liberated.

"Now it's my turn!" she said. She began talking about our life together from her perspective. She said that she had never felt secure in my love and that she wanted my love more than anything. She was always afraid I would leave her and not return. She blamed me for the breakup with her father, and she felt abandoned by him and angry with me for sending him away. In her feelings of abandonment by her father, she clung more tightly to me. She wanted more from me. I, in my ignorance, anger, and frustration, had been unable to understand her feelings or soothe her anxiety of being abandoned. She felt alone, neglected, unimportant, and unloved and unlovable. She felt I had let her down. She felt abandoned by me too in many ways. And in truth, in my ignorance and pain, I had emotionally abandoned my child.

Our walk ended with our crying and hugging. We faced our feelings and we survived. We knew that we had just begun and still had more to do, but we had embarked on a long awaited journey. In releasing our feelings, my daughter and I had begun to communicate, and I wanted it to continue forever. Susan is and always has been the most important part of my life even though I didn't know how to show my love. Until now our relationship was fraught with disappointment and anger. I knew as she was growing up I was not the kind of storybook mother that she was looking for because, in reality, I didn't want to be. I felt guilty for that too. But after all of these years, I was confident that if Susan and I continued to communicate, I would be the mother that would show love freely anytime she needed me to show her my love. I also knew I loved her more than anything in this world and I was willing to show that love as I was learning. In short, I was willing and ready to have the relationship that we both always wanted and didn't know how to achieve earlier and before cancer.

I was eager to release the guilt and pain that I had carried, and she was ready to release her anger and expectations of me. And we had cancer to thank for creating this miracle. We returned home exhausted and spent but happy that we had finally been able to deal with our pain and fears. A few days later, I returned to Richmond to prepare for the next surgery.

Step Fourteen

Trust the Boss

Our deepest fear is not that we are inadequate,
Our deepest fear is that we are powerful beyond measure.
It is our light, not our darkness that frightens us.
We ask ourselves, who am I to be brilliant, gorgeous,
talented, and fabulous?
Actually, who are you not to be?
You are a child of God.
Your playing small doesn't serve the world.
There's nothing enlightened about shrinking so that
other people won't feel insecure around you.
We are born to make manifest the glory of God that is
within us.
It's not just in some of us, it's in everyone.
And as we let our own light shine, we unconsciously
give other people permission to do the same.
And we are liberated from our own fears, our presence
automatically liberates others.

Marianne Williamson, *A Return to Love*

Step 14: This is perhaps the most difficult step to write because it relies on faith alone. However the good news is that this step is far easier to accomplish than all that I have asked of you so far. This chapter is about the God I have come to know, appreciate and love; the Inner Voice that loves me, reassures me, and guides me daily.

Who and what is God really? There are many differing opinions existing in the world. And why is this last chapter about God? This chapter, in my opinion, contains the last and most significant component of my personal process for continuance and preservation of the peace that I have found, and hopefully the process that you have begun with the help of this book. It could also be the most controversial and divisive because there are so many conflicting beliefs and skepticism about God. Two questions that I asked of you earlier were "Do you believe in God?" and "Do you believe that God is within you?" I don't know your answers, but I will give you my reality because I do know *my* answers. What follows is my own truth and my own beliefs based on my many mind-blowing, remarkable and surprising experiences over the last fifteen years.

Yes, there is a God. It is sureness for me after years of uncertainty. Since I have relinquished judgment, condemnation of myself and others, and practice forgiveness daily, I have the ability to hear a gentle and wise internal voice consistently, anytime I ask, and the advice and answers I receive are beyond reproach. Sometimes I hear a voice in my head, and other times I speak the words for the voice aloud to me after I've asked for help. I wish I could take credit for being so wise and munificent, but I must give credit where it is due.

The advice I hear is a constant. It is loving, compassionate, benevolent, has a sense of humor, and is always appropriate to the situation. This is not the human way, and I know I am still human because I still find myself judging frequently. The only difference now is that I quickly recognize the judgment, release it, and then forgive myself. The voice I hear never wavers from love, is always there for me, and always helps me to help myself and help others in my work.

My point is that I am not special; I am human, made and still make many mistakes, and if I can hear this voice, so can you. I assure you that if you clear your mind of the negativity that is carries, literally all desires and results are possible. The voice also reminds me that it doesn't matter if I make mistakes because I am human. I must only forgive myself and continue to remember that I am a child of God. It also tells me that what *does* matter is what I do when I err. What does matter is how I feel about myself and what I learn from my mistakes. I am not mentally ill; I do hear a voice and I do have a few strange and unusual stories to tell that made me a believer prior to and after having cancer. I actually have had many mystical experiences since then but will start with the first two. Until those experiences, I had nothing to affirm that God existed.

Back in the '80s when my husband and I were newly married, we had a reoccurring problem that we argued about frequently. Bob tends to ignore issues so whenever I would attempt to talk about the problem and give him my opinion; he would get angry and walk away, leaving us both frustrated and angry. This morning was no different. We were in the bedroom, the issue was raised, and he walked out of the room, leaving me sitting on the bed, crying. I sat there for a few moments feeling very alone. I silently asked God for help. I asked Him to help me see this differently and handle this differently. Within two or three minutes, I stood up, walked out to the kitchen, with no idea of what I was prepared to say. As I reached the kitchen, my husband's irritated facial expression said, "Okay, here we go again. I don't want to talk about this." I ignored the look on his face and started speaking and suddenly I was asking questions and making suggestions that amazed me. I felt like I was above myself, observing and saying all the right words. I could see the look on his face change from one of irritation to one of interest and caring. He was listening and his reaction was different than it had ever been on this subject. The observer part of me was saying, "Wow, this is great stuff. Where is it coming from?" I felt split, delighted, surprised by my different approach and the words coming out of my mouth and amazed by the immediate change in his reaction. It was surreal, but whatever or whoever helped me that day resolved forever a long-standing issue in about five minutes. I asked for help and received it immediately, the first time of many.

The second incident was one that I never shared for years, fearful that people might think me crazy. I was the director of a New York State agency with ninety-five people under my care and direction. And with ninety-five people to deal with daily, there were always a few who complained and didn't agree with my decisions as director. In those days I was a big time people pleaser and I frequently had my "feelings hurt" because I took the complainers personally. This was almost a daily occurrence, and one night, on my ride home from work, I was crying, feeling sad and sorry for myself. I could not cry with people around, but I did allow myself to cry when I was alone.

I talked out loud to myself in my car frequently, and this night I said, "I wish I had someone like me to talk to." (I had always been a counselor to my friends but had no one to help me.) Loudly and clearly, I heard my own voice say strongly, "You do." Shocked by the answer I never expected, I responded with my tearful voice, "I do? Who?" A strong, calm, reassuring voice answered, "You." My tearful voice and my strong, wise, calm voice continued a dialogue for about twenty minutes. The "voice" was the wisest advisor/counselor I had ever been exposed to, and it continued to ask me questions that I answered. It helped me process the day's problems and guided me in organizing a plan for the future in similar instances. It asked me many questions like, "What would you like to come of this?" "What would you like to do differently?" And I answered the questions. From that day on, I had a wise therapist to assist every time I needed help. It is the same voice that I "hear" today. I have only to ask to receive. These are only two of the countless times that I have received and continue to receive help. The more I practiced, the more immediate was the response, always ready with straightforward, practical, spiritual assistance. I grew to trust it would always be there and I began to feel less and less alone and more and more protected. Again, if I can access this type of guidance so can you. But you must remember to ask for help to see a situation differently. I believe God gave us free will so He will not interfere with our free will unless we ask for help. I asked and I received.

Surveys and studies show that the majority of people believe in a higher intelligence that created all life. There are so many names for God: Higher Intelligence, Jehovah, Abraham, Creator, Buddha, Allah, higher wisdom, intuition, higher power, Brahma, the Light, the Force, Supreme Being, source, the Universe, the Tao, Zeus and multiple Greek gods, and many others. For purposes of simplicity, I use God because for me, it covers all that espouses love. I also use the male pronoun when I speak of Him because it is easier than writing He/She, but I know that God is neither a he nor a she. God is an indescribable being that I cannot even imagine. I do believe that God is pure love but I have no idea what pure love "looks" like. I do, however receive an occasional glimmer and *know the feeling* of pure love, at least sometimes, and with increasing frequency. I do feel gratitude and pure joy frequently.

I believe, as do most people, that we are all a part of God as our Creator. Therefore we are linked forever to each other and to God. And when I asked, I was told by the Voice that we are all one. The inner wisdom or intuition from God resides within our spirit or soul and is always available to guide us. We don't hear it clearly because the many inner children repeat and shout the words of admonishment we received as children. That and additional negative programming formed our egos and our opinions. There are multiple examples used throughout this book.

For thousands of years, spiritual leaders have provided basic tenets to live a peaceful, happy life. Two thousand years ago, Jesus walked this earth with a powerful, simple message for living an actualized life. He also said, "You can do all that I can do and more." I trust him and I believe him. Five hundred years earlier, Buddha, in his teachings, used almost the same words as Jesus. Each gave simple messages of unconditional love and forgiveness of self and others. These principles are widely accepted and preached today, but not actualized in most societies. Why is it that so many of us are unable to apply these concepts consistently in our lives? The answer is basic and simple to me. It is because we don't know how to love and accept ourselves unconditionally, so we look outside, project our guilt and blame onto someone else when we hurt and through judgment we make it impossible for us to give or to accept unconditional love on a consistent basis.

> *"But the greatest menace to our civilization today is the conflict between giant organized systems of self-righteousness—each system only too delighted to find that the other is wicked—each only too glad that the sins give it the pretext for still deeper hatred and animosity."*
>
> Herbert Butterfield

I happen to agree with Butterfield's statement but I also believe that more importantly, through self-love we can overcome all obstacles to peace. I also believe there would be fewer obstacles to peace if everyone was able to achieve self-love. Is God punishing? I believe not. I think God loves all His children and God being pure Love in my opinion would never punish. We were given free will, and we create our life by our choices and by our perceptions. We do the judging and the punishing. God doesn't. God is pure love, and pure love does not have an opposite.

It is always easily apparent and obvious to recognize

when others are in the wrong. It's much more difficult to recognize your own role in creating the problems you confront. It is easier to judge others because there is no fear present in judging others. When you judge another you don't have to examine your behavior. The other person must make the changes necessary for peace. It is much more difficult and fear inducing to take responsibility and change your self.

The more we focus on others, the less responsibility we take for our choices and we create our life unconsciously. It is much more comfortable to see how others need to change, than to look at how we need to change. Mahatma Gandhi said, *"We must become the change we want to see in this world."* Taking responsibility for your choices, your actions and your life is the only path to transformation; it must start with you. You choose your perceptions. You choose your thoughts and emotions. You choose your actions. And those choices create your life as you experience it. So on your path to self-love and self-awareness, choose consciously, carefully and wisely.

However, because of our IC's, the past has proven that peace is temporary at best and there is always a victim and an aggressor. To my way of thinking, changing how you see the world implies relinquishing judgment. It suggests practicing forgiveness and to do both you must possess self- love. Our track record as human beings is not impressive in either case and I hold the IC's within accountable for our obstacles because our IC's exist within us without our awareness. With the awareness that you have developed in this process, you are fully capable of loving each IC. You also know how to give them the love they have been looking for all of your life. You can raise them properly, uniting yourself into the maturity of a happy, healthy, peaceful and self-loving person as God intended. It takes vigilance in your thoughts but if you have made it thus far, you are remarkable.

> *"To put the world right in order, we must first put the nation in order; to put the nation in order we must first put the family in order; to put the family in order, we must first cultivate our personal life; we must first set our hearts straight."*
>
> Confucius

What Confucius is saying is that we need to know who we are and why we behave as we do so we can set our hearts straight before we are able to make choices from our heart. I believe we must explore and cultivate our similarities, not our differences. September 11, 2001, was the first time that a terrorist event of such magnitude occurred in this country. Was this meant to be a wake up call for our country, which just happens to be the world leader? If so, the wake up call was meant for every individual living in our county. When Jesus preached, his message was simple. Love one another and treat others as you would like to be treated. If someone steals from you, give him more. Everyone is created equal. Each person is on earth for a reason.

Jesus gave his love to those whom he felt needed it most: outcasts, sinners, tax collectors, and prostitutes, those that most people chose to judge. He said, "Let those who are without sin, cast the first stone," as the crowd was condemning a woman believed to be cheating on her husband. His message was clear. No one has a right to judge and that he loved everyone. So much so that he refused to defend himself and his life when he knew he would be crucified. His message was love for all and that begins with self-love.

> *"The value of life lies not in the length of days, but in the use we make of them; a man may live long yet live very little."*
>
> Montaigne, Essays, 1580

When I am in fear and frightened, my personal choice and immediate relief is to release the fear to God. Release of all fear, for me, came permanently when I finally surrendered my life to God, in 2003 when I attended a Buddhist retreat in Santa Fe, New Mexico. I was moving to Reno, Nevada, soon and was happy and ready to go. It was a silent retreat, and the first morning, the leader, after an hours discussion told us that she had Multiple Sclerosis and that she would be with us in the mornings but she would then withdraw to her room to rest so she could take care of herself. She said she would be unavailable to us except for the morning talks.

At noon, right after morning meditation and before lunch, I went to my room to use the bathroom. When I looked into the toilet bowl, I saw that it was filled with thick, bright red blood. As a two-time cancer survivor, I gasped and was immediately engulfed with the same terrifying fear I felt with both cancer findings. I panicked and ran directly to the leader's room. She opened the door and started to remind me that she needed this time alone, but at this time, I was an experienced full-time counselor, and I knew I just needed someone calm to help me get on the right path. I was so terrified, I forgot about God. I asked her to give me five minutes. She invited me in, I told her my background and about the blood. She gave me no answers, just asked, "What would you say if you were advising someone now?" I told her I would advise they take time for meditation and go off into the woods to write and allow their fears to surface as soon as possible. She said, "That is exactly what you need to do."

So I took my *A Course in Miracles* book, a chair, and a box of Kleenex off into the woods and sat down on the chair. I began sobbing uncontrollably and just allowed the fear to flow through me and permitted myself to cry as long as I needed. I wept for at least twenty to thirty minutes without stopping. When I was exhausted and could cry no more, I opened my book to a random page knowing that I would find an answer and I did. On the open page, I read in big letters, "Oh you of little faith."

At that point, all that I ever learned from both cancers came flowing back into me, and I remembered that I had control over nothing but my mind, my choices, and my feelings. That day for the first time, I surrendered myself to God. I realized that nothing, no person, no car, no house, no city, no travel, no job, nothing in this world was important except my relationship with God. And on that day I was able to release my attachment to everyone and every "thing" that existed on this earth. I surrendered myself completely to God, telling myself that I was going to be "okay no matter what happened." And I decided that even if I died from whatever caused the bleeding that I would still and always be okay because my mind would always be with God. My body was temporary, but my mind was eternal and would be with

God. I found great peace in that belief and to this day I have never wavered in that belief.

Since that day, whenever I recognize my feelings as worry or fear based, I surrender to God, give him my panic and stop thinking about whatever dread I may be carrying. This is not avoidance or escape. It is the relinquishment of a situation that I recognize I have no control over, and I give it to the inner voice I frequently hear within me for resolution. My first thought when I recognize fear (which is still frequent as I am, after all, a full-blooded Italian) is to determine if there are any actions I can undertake to help the situation (to be interpreted as taking responsibility for myself). If I find there is any action that will help, I take the necessary action. If it helps, I am grateful.

If it doesn't and if fear is still present after that, I talk to God, and surrender my will and my life to God and ask for any help He can give me to be peaceful and serene. Then I listen carefully, receive the answers, and do as I am told. Sometimes I am lightly guided to "butt out of someone else's business," or told to "Lighten up" when I am hanging onto fear. Sometimes it is given with humor but the direction is always appropriate, gentle and kind. Usually when I am scared, what I literally hear is, "Stop worrying, stay in the present, and practice what you teach. You teach what you need to learn." In cases of judgment, I will often hear, "Give it up, Ali. Relax and let go of what doesn't feel good."

Not too long ago, when I was busy being disappointed by others, I heard, "If you spend a lot of time being disappointed in others, you will feel disappointed most of the time." It made me smile because the solution was so plain and simple and absolutely right. It usually is and often makes me laugh at myself. Yet it never gives me advice that creates more problems. It always gives me resolution for myself and others if I do as I am told. The answers and advice are always straightforward and uncomplicated and are usually given with a sense of humor. God frequently makes me laugh especially at myself. Secretly though, I really believe it is Jesus talking to me, since he promised to be there for all of us when we are in need. I see these as gentle lessons which always precede more difficult warnings. I try to pay attention to the gentle ones now to help me avoid the harsher lessons of life. I have found that this works for me so I am grateful and vigilant of the emergence of the gentler ones. I can report to you that it works.

There is great hope in self-awareness and self-love. Self-awareness and self-love is the only means to convert your thoughts and allow change without the worry of a mysterious, unfamiliar and unknown. Once you develop your awareness through the process in this book you will never be the same. A trust and belief begins to form within you that unlocks the unconscious and dissipates the negativity in your mind. As the negativity dissolves, your trust becomes faith and you begin to recognize and experience success in your endeavors. Once you experience the joy that this process brings, you have reclaimed your power and are connected with the God within us all.

Our body talks to us all of the time. Every pain we have is a message from our body. This alone is reason enough to discover what lies hidden deep within us. Health, love and happiness! Get started today. Today is the beginning of the rest of your life.

The following quotation is from *A Course in Miracles* and seems pertinent to peace in every aspect of living.

> *"Seek not to change the world, rather seek to change how you see the world."*

These words are capable of transforming your world. Transforming your world means consciously and responsibly converting your thoughts and actions minute by minute, hour by hour, day by day and situation by situation. To do so places you in control of your happiness. Peace will no longer be elusive. You have abandoned the victim role and have removed the majority of your obstacles to your peace. You will have achieved the highest and most rewarding success. Congratulations and I wish you love and peace in your present and future.

> *"There is a place in you where there is perfect peace. There is a place in you where nothing is impossible. There is a place in you where the strength of God abides."*
>
> *A Course in Miracles* WB76, 1.6.7.8

People Pleasing

By: Connor Monaghan

It's being a people pleasing boy
in a world of spoiled
and people PLEASED people,
feeling as though I am always
conforming to everyone's
every whim.
It's feeling as though I am the
only one capable
of enduring the pain and suffering
and of lacking
oh so comforting satisfaction.
My mind says no
and loses due to the compulsive component it lacks,
my heart says yes
and wins due to the compulsive component it is blessed.

I do not suffer from a wounded heart,
but an entrapped mind,
unable to voice its opinion,
or enjoy what it desires.
Light dwells at the end of the tunnel,
my heart grows stronger as my mind sharpens,
it gives less to conformity everyday,
while never losing the blessing of its compulsive nature.
A strong heart and a strong mind
combined have a wisdom comparable to a sage,
but like a sages' wisdom,
this is not attainable without sacrifice.
My heart and mind are on a journey
towards the gift of enlightenment and
inevitable rest.

(Connor Monaghan is the 18-year-old grandson of Ali McDowell. This is his first poem.)

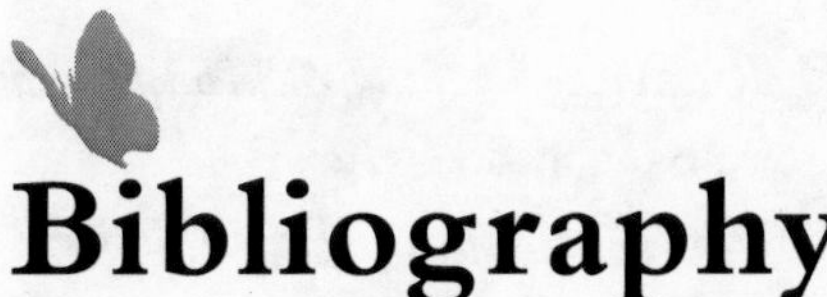

Bibliography

A Course in Miracles. Combined Volume. Tiburon, California: Foundation for Inner Peace, 1992 (original ed. 1975)

Benson, Herbert, *Timeless Healing,* Fireside

Brandon, Nathaniel, *Six Pillars of Self Esteem,* New York: Bantam Books

Chopra, Deepak, MD, *Quantum Healing: Exploring the Frontiers of Mind/Body Medicine.* New York: Bantam Books, 1989

———, *The Seven Spiritual Laws of Success.* San Rafael, CA: Amber-Allen Publishing, 1994

———, *Unconditional Life,* New York: Bantam Books

———, *Ageless Body, Timeless Mind,* New York: Bantam Books

Covey, Steven, *First Things First,* New York: Simon & Schuster

———, *Seven Habits of Highly Effective People,* New York: Simon & Schuster

Dass, Ram, *Journey of Awakening,* New York: Bantam Books

De Mello, Anthony, *A Way to Love,* New York: Bantam-Doubleday, 1993

Dossey, Larry, MD, *Recovering the Soul: A Scientific and Spiritual Search,* New York: Bantam Books, 1989

———, *Healing Words,* New York: Harper Collins Publishers, 1993

Dr. Julian Whitaker's Health & Healing, A Monthly Publication, Potomac, MD: Phillips Publishing

Fanning, Patrick, McKay, Matthew, *Self Esteem, Second Edition*, New Harbinger Publications

Hay, Louise, *The Power Is Within You,* Hay House

———, *You Can Heal Your Life,* Hay House

Hall, L.Michael & Bodenhamer, Bobby G., *Mind Lines, Nuero-Semantics Publications,* 2005

Harvard Women's Health Watch, A Monthly Publication, Boston, Ma: Harvard Health Publications

Hawkes, Joyce Whiteley, Attria Books & BeyondWords Publication, 2006

Hicks, Esther and Jerry, *The Law of Attraction*, Hay House Inc, 2006

Horney, Karen, W.W.Norton & Company, 1945

The Holy Bible. The International Version. Grand Rapids, Mich.: Zondervan Bible Publishers, 1978

Kornfield, Jack, *A Path With Heart,*

Kornfield, Jack, Goldstein, Joseph, *Seeking The Heart of Wisdom,* Shambala Publishers

Le Shan, Lawrence, *You Can Fight For Your Life, Emotional Factors In the Causation of Cancer*

Mate, Gabor, When the Body Says No; Understanding the Cost of Hidden Stress

Mayo Clinic Health Letter, A Monthly Publication, Rochester, MN: Mayo Foundation for Medical Education and Research, A Subsidiary of Mayo Foundation

McCullough, Christopher J., Woods Mann, Robert, *Managing Your Anxiety,* Berkley Books

McDonald, Kathleen, *How to Meditate,* Wisdom Publications

Moore, Thomas, *Care of the Soul,* Harper Collins

Morra, Marion & Potts, Eve, *Triumph, Getting Back To Normal When You Have Cancer*, Avon Books

Myss, Caroline, Shealy, C. Norman MD, *Creation of Health,* Stillpoint Publishing

Myss, Caroline, *Anatomy of a Spirit,* Stillpoint Publishing

Northrup, Christine, MD, *Women's Health, Women's Wisdom,* New York: Bantam Books

Ornish, Dean, MD, *Reversing Heart Disease,* First Ballantine Books

Pearsall, Paul, *Super Immunity, Master Your Emotions and Improve Your Health,* Ballantine Books

Peurifoy, Reneau Z, *Anxiety, Phobias and Panic,* Warner Books

Saint Germain. *The I Am Discourses.* Schaumburg, Ill.: St. Germain Press, 1984

Sapolsky, Robert M., *Why Zebra's Don't Get Ulcers,* W.H.Freeman & Company, 1998

Shandler, Nina, *Estrogen, The Natural Way,* New York: Random House, 1997

Siegel, Bernie S. MD, *How to Live Between Office Visits.* New York: Harper Collins Publishers, 1993

———. *Love, Medicine and Miracles.* New York: Harper Collins Publishers, 1986

———. *Peace, Love and Healing.* New York: Harper Collins Publishers, 1989

Sinatra, Stephen, MD, *Heart Sense, A Monthly Publication,* Potomac, MD: Phillips Publishing, Inc

Simonton, O. Carl, MD, Matthews Simonton, Stephanie, Creighton, James, *Getting Well Again,* New York: Bantam Books

Simonton, O. Carl, Reid Henson. *The Healing Journey: Restoring Health and Harmony to Body, Mind, and Spirit.* New York: Bantam Books, 1992

Sylvest, Vernon M., *The Formula, Four Keys to Unfolding Your Full Potential, Who Gets Sick,*

Walsch, Neale Donald, *Conversations with God, Book One,*

———, *Conversations with God, Book Three*

Who Gets Well, Who Is Unhappy, Who Is Happy and Why, Fairfield, Iowa: Sunstar Publishing Ltd, 1999

Wapnick, Kenneth, Ph.D., *Absence From Felicity,* Foundation For A Course In Miracles

Wapnick, Kenneth Ph.D., *All Are Chosen,* Foundation For A Course In Miracles

Wapnick, Kenneth PhD, *Few Choose to Listen,* Foundation For A Course In Miracles

Wapnick, Kenneth PhD, *Forgiveness and Jesus,* Foundation For A Course In Miracles

Weil, Andrew, MD. *Spontaneous Healing*. New York: Alfred A. Knopf, 1995

Women's Health Advisor, A Monthly Publication, Weill Medical College of Cornell University, Palm Coast, Fl: Torstar Publications

Who Gets Well, Who Is Unhappy, Who Is Happy and Why, Fairfield, Iowa: Sunstar Publishiing Ltd., 1999

Worst, Judith, Necessary Losses, Simon & Schuster

Tapes

Conversations with God, Book One, Volume 1, 2, *and* 3, Neale Donald Walsch, Audio Literature

Energy of Anatomy, The Science of Personal Power, Spirituality and Health, Carolyn Myss, Sounds True

Freedom, Expanding Personal Freedom Tapes, Stuart Wilde

Igniting Intuition, Unearthing Body Genius, Christine Northrup, M.D., Mona Lisa Schultz, M.D., PhD

I Want The Peace of God, Kenneth Wapnik, Ph.D, Foundation For A Course In Miracles

Love, Medicine & Miracles, Bernie Siegel, M.D., Harper Audio

Marianne Williamson Live, Marianne Williamson, Nightingale Conant

Meditations for Peace of Mind, Bernie S. Siegel, M.D., Hay House

8 *Meditations for Optimum Health*, Andrew Weil, M.D., UPAYA

Meditations for Healing Your Inner Child, Bernie Siegel, M.D., Hay House

Peace, Love and Healing, The Body, Mind & Path to Self-Healing: An Exploration, Bernie Siegel, MD, and Caldron

Sickness and Healing, Kenneth Wapnick, PhD., Foundation For A Course In Miracles

Teacher of Forgiveness, Kenneth Wapnick, PhD., Foundation For A Course In Miracles

Why People Don't Heal and How They Can, Carolyn Myss, Great Lakes training Associates

Articles

Emotional Processing & Physical Health, emotional processing.org

Grodsky, Lynn. *Approaching a Theory of Emotion: An Interview with Candace Pert, PhD,* primal-page.com

Norton, Amy. *Happiness May Be Good for Your Health,* reuters.com, January 3, 2008

Youngmee, Kim & Deci, Edward L & Zuckerman, Miron. *The Development of the Self-Regulation of Withholding Negative Emotions Questionnaire,* Sage Publications, 2002

Quinlan, Jay. *Psychoneuroimmunology,* nfnlp.com

Internet Sources

The Daily Guru, thedailyguru.com

Inner Self Daily Inspiration, http//innerself.com

The author welcomes comments and questions from readers. You can email her at ali@alicemcdowell.com, or write her at Ali McDowell, PO Box 1001, Kingston, TN 37763-1001. For more information about workshops, newsletter or lectures, visit her website at ALICEMCDOWELL.COM

listen|imagine|view|experience

AUDIO BOOK DOWNLOAD INCLUDED WITH THIS BOOK!

In your hands you hold a complete digital entertainment package. Besides purchasing the paper version of this book, this book includes a free download of the audio version of this book. Simply use the code listed below when visiting our website. Once downloaded to your computer, you can listen to the book through your computer's speakers, burn it to an audio CD or save the file to your portable music device (such as Apple's popular iPod) and listen on the go!

How to get your free audio book digital download:

1. Visit www.tatepublishing.com and click on the e|LIVE logo on the home page.
2. Enter the following coupon code: 16b2-2b97-a663-ebde-5b60-75fd-18e5-cc5c
3. Download the audio book from your e|LIVE digital locker and begin enjoying your new digital entertainment package today!